FAR FRO1

Far From Tipperary

An Army Chaplain's
Adventure of Faith

Memoirs of
THE VERY REV. IVAN D NEILL
CB, OBE, MA(Cantab)

Copyright © Ivan D Neill 2000

First published 2000

Published by the author:
York House, 194 High Street
Uckfield
TN22 1RD
England

ISBN: 0 9539491 0 9

Distributed by Christian Literature Crusade
51, The Dean, Alresford, Hants SO24 9BJ.

Designed and produced for the publisher by
Bookprint Creative Services, P.O. Box 827, BN21 3YJ, England.
Printed in Great Britain.

This book is dedicated
to those with whom I served in the Army
and civilian life, not forgetting those who had
the faithfulness to criticise, and
sometimes rebuke, me.

CONTENTS

FOREWORD

The memoirs which you are about to read recount the life-story of a man of faith whose life span has covered the greater part of the twentieth century. The significance of the account is that the narrator played his part throughout that turbulent, faith-destroying, secularising century, addressing it with a faith unquestioning and unwavering, infectious and warm, a faith steadfast and certain.

Born in the years before the horrors of the Great War of 1914–18, we quickly move through his early home life, his years at school and at Cambridge, to his notable contribution to the Army Chaplains' Department, which he was eventually to head as Chaplain General.

It was the war years of 1939–45 which bore the first powerful witness to his ministry. We read of his addressing and helping the vast numbers of those young men, many with little or no faith, face to face with violent death before they had had any experience of life, hurled into a situation they could neither cope with nor understand, casualties of a faithless, secularised, lost society. We read of his addressing men about to die in battle, of the painful numbering and recording of those who went ungrudgingly, and spent their young lives for us; their reverent committal to the grave; their account to the loved ones at home. We recall the unforgettable cost of our deliverance from pagan totalitarianism, whereby I now sit in peace and quiet to write these words and reflect on the heartbreak at the heart of things. In all these things Ivan ever strove to kindle faith in the hearts and minds of men to enable them to sustain themselves through the horrors they neither created nor deserved.

On retirement as Chaplain General, he was called to Sheffield, as Vicar of Sheffield and Provost of the Cathedral. At that time, my being Professor of Biblical Studies at the University, the then Bishop of Sheffield, dear John Taylor, had the happy inspiration to create the post of Canon Theologian at the Cathedral. He installed me there, where, as a member of Chapter, I worked with Ivan throughout his years at Sheffield, happy to serve and support his ministry.

It was here that Ivan exercised perhaps his finest and fullest ministry. First, it was a ministry of the Word. None will ever forget his soft warm voice expounding the Word of God, that it may speak to and within the heart and mind of the hearer, creating and building faith. He was always worth hearing. He did tell us about God in Christ reconciling man to Himself. Furthermore, it was always a care and cure of souls. Beyond his pastoral care of the congregation, his ministry to the civic life, to the Master Cutler and his Company, above all, to that unique and fine body, the Church burgesses, was deeply impressive and universally appreciated.

He was always a joy to meet, for his devoted ministry was ever spiced with a characteristic, warm Irish humour.

It was during his Sheffield ministry that his wife, Pat, came into her own, in that she shared his ministry at a public level which she could not while Ivan was in the Army. She held a redoubtable, evangelical faith and a mind of her own, which she would give expression to with clarity and conviction. Pat was an outstanding and kind hostess, and was a rock-like support to Ivan. It seemed to me, and to many others, a perfect marriage; they seemed like one person. When the severity of the Sheffield climate strained Pat's health beyond endurance, and cut short their ministry to us in Sheffield, sorrow filled our hearts, for we all felt the finality of it all. When I later was to face the responsibility of preaching the sermon at her memorial service at St. Paul's Cathedral to a devout congregation supported by fine music, I felt we were committing to God a much loved soul He had already taken to Himself.

Ivan still continues his ministry, as we would want him to do. He never did retire. God will retire him in His own time, and that will be retirement indeed.

He leaves his footprints on the sands of time. They are worthy of note. It was to this end his family and friends requested that these memoirs be written before they were forgotten, and to this end, I commend them.

The Rev[d]. Canon Professor James Atkinson
MA, MLitt, DTh, DD

ACKNOWLEDGEMENTS

Very special thanks to Patricia, my daughter, who typed and often improved on the manuscript, to Robert, my son, and to Clifford Dann, my son-in-law, for their most helpful comments and suggestions.

Chapter I
EARLIEST DAYS

'To Robert Richard Neill of Templeharry Rectory Church of Ireland Clergyman and to Bessie Montrose, formerly Purdon' so was my birth registered as having occurred in Templeharry Rectory on tenth day of July 1912. Templeharry was on the border of what was then Kings County – now Offaly – but was actually in the County of Tipperary, and in the district of Birr.

Memories of those early days are scant and possibly clothed with family narratives told in later years. The rectory stood in its own grounds and I can still remember being laid in a hammock for afternoon rest and in the shade of a tree which only spelt loneliness to me. Nannies came and went. One was dismissed for chastising my elder brother with nettles although she maintained that Robin had fallen into a nettle bed. I remember being frightened of motor cars then; horses, carriages and pony traps were much more friendly things. My father used a pony and trap and to ride with him was to remember the repeated salutations from ditches almost always occupied by men folk. I still remember Mrs

Armitage of the village shop in her blue dress with white spots and the characteristic carbolic smell of her shop. She and the elderly squire from the castle regarded each other with distaste until he moved across the church one day and held out his hand to her before receiving Holy Communion. He was my Godfather.

I still hold memories of the drawing room in the Templeharry rectory, half of which was 'up one step', and of the rule that one must not 'not like' one's food unless one wanted a larger helping: and I just remember Albert – a sort of boots handyman – who used to help himself to the maids' sugar. My father laid a trap for him – but this was a family story. My father was a good amateur photographer and he made as though he had used the maids' sugar basin for 'his chemicals'. Alfred, who always made free with the maids' sugar, had tipped the contents of this sugar basin into the pot of tea he was making for himself and was horrified to be told that 'the master's chemicals' were missing. He was reprimanded in my father's study and advised of the possibility of acute stomach pains. He begged a preventative pill and accepted a cascara which he had to suck to its bitter end and not to swallow. On one occasion, and because of the complaints of the maids, he was told to take a bath. He consulted the maids – 'The master says I must take a bath. What might that mean?'

When I was three years old my father was appointed Rector of St Peter's Cork. The Rectory in Cork was opposite a large gateway by which one would have approached the University had the bridge across a stream not been broken down. Between that gateway and the rectory was the

'Western Road' on one side of which ran the Blarney train, and in the centre of which ran a tramway which passed the approach to the gaol, which was half a mile away. Just past the Rectory the metalled road gave way to earth – a 'dirt road'.

During those early days in Tipperary and Cork I know that it was a disappointment to my parents that I had not been born a girl. My hair, which then was very fair, reached down to my waist and I invariably wore a 'tunic' (a skirted coat style garment then often worn by children) and these must have been green in colour for I hated that colour for a long long time. My parents were delighted to hear their new parishion-ers extol the charm of the rectory children – two delightful boys and their little sister. They often in later years recalled this as an amusing tale, but never realised that I was more hurt than amused. They had a very enlarged photograph of me sitting in a basket chair but, this having become an attic relic, I managed to destroy it in my Cambridge days.

To us boys, for we lived in Cork for seven or more years, the train and tram lines provided great entertainment after we had discovered where our father kept his cartridges. I never remember his shooting activities, perhaps an urban parish made too many demands but I remember our delight to see trams stop and the driver and conductor walk round and round to see what had caused an explosion so like a gun shot. A cartridge case flattened into the tramway did not catch the eye!

My two elder brothers and I went to a kindergarten school run by a Miss Bergen and boarded there at such times as the arrivals of a younger brother and a sister were due. We were five in all. At Miss Bergen's school we were put through our

paces with caring discipline and one punishment I remember
was to have to butter both sides of our bread – and this was
war time! The punishment was that we had to tell whoever
asked why we so buttered our bread just why we did it, and
what it was we had done wrong. Every day school ended with
a homily of some sort and then we all sang the list of the books
of the Bible to the tune 'Sun of my soul' (Hursley). In those
days for 'lesser' work we worked on slate mounted in a
wooden frame and we wrote out our sums etc. with slate
pencils whose squeak could be horrific. My teeth are, even
now, on edge as I recall it, some 80 and more years later.

The rectory bordered on to the Bandstand in Cork, an area
lying between the Western Road and the Mardyke Walk and
a choice place for ambushing police vehicles as they roared
down the road, searchlights beaming out – towards the city
itself. A much loved aunt who was one of the original voluntary helpers of Miss Sandes in her Soldiers' Home-work, once
was unwise enough to say she would like to see some of the
'action' the papers wrote about. Within minutes there was a
shot and the most horrific cries. A young couple in the
Bandstand area in their embrace has been suspected of terrorist activities and the man's brains had been blown out by the
shot fired; the girl was hysterical.

Those were days when we abandoned our beds for mat-
tresses on the floor because of the danger of bullets coming
through the windows (we never had any, other than on the
outside walls). A story was told of my eldest brother who had
taken refuge with this aunt who was staying with us on
holiday from the Fermoy Soldier's Home. 'Auntie', he said
against the noise of cross fire around us, 'is this what you call

an engagement?' 'Yes, dear'. 'Then what must a marriage be like?' For some few nights the rectory became haven to seven families whose houses were burnt down by the 'Black & Tans' on the terrible night they burnt out St. Patrick's Street and some of the South Mall. We also had an amusing couple, a clown and his wife, who had experienced conversion and who were in temporary financial straits. (I understood he was Dan Leno). He painted what were to me attractive oil paintings on the bathroom wall, and I remember his chasing his wife round the house (backstairs and front) with a wet paint brush.

Then came the time of bewilderment. The Garrison Commander of Cork asked if all loyalists would display a Union Jack in support of the forces of law and order – and within days the British troops were withdrawn.

I remember the workman weeping as he painted green the red letterbox at our gate and all the postage stamps being overprinted in Irish but printed the other way up in the hope that they would be used 'right way up' for the Irish who then would have turned our King's head upside down. I also remember the burnings down of many prominent peoples' houses around Cork, and the 'troubles' between the 'Free State' and the Republican armies. We were holidaying in Youghal, Co. Cork – Sir Walter Raleigh's seat when he was British Resident there – when the 'Free State' landed from a gun boat to flush the republicans out of Cork. Eager recruiting took place on the Quay before the battle joined in mid morning and we were caught in the cross fire because of our stupidity of having enjoyed sight-seeing. My mother saw some of the recruiting in progress and was highly amused by what she heard. 'O Gawd, look, there is Mike. Mike, it's a good lad ye are for joining up. I hope ye have a good funeral.'

The period known as 'The Troubled Times' should perhaps be enlarged upon but I will be the first to admit that I am raising controversial issues.

There had always been a rebellious voice maintaining that Ireland had never been fully conquered by England. A sizeable area round Dublin had been subjected and those living within it were described as 'living within the pale' and in addition there were estates granted by the Crown, mostly in the time of Queen Elizabeth I, which were given to families strong enough to discipline the 'native' residents, thus creating a festering sore. Many many Irishman 'joined up' in World War I, some into long established gallant Irish regiments, others into English Corps and Services, but the rebellious element saw the opportunity of breaking from the 'English yoke'. Some forty people armed with tools of their trades – pitchforks, spades, crowbars, spanners and wrenches, stormed the General Post Office on Sackville Street on 24 April 1916 and the Republican Army was born.

British forces were finally withdrawn in 1922 and the IRA (Irish Republican Army) was divided over the status of Ulster. The 'Irish Free State' (Sinn Fein – ourselves alone) and the Republicans were at war, the one with the other and it was a savage war. The 'Black and Tans', of very questionable repute, came on the scenes during the height of the rebellion in the year 1920. The Royal Irish Constabulary (the Police) had had as much as they could take. The Black and Tans were largely British ex-servicemen out of work and some, by joining up again to serve in Ireland, were evading prison sentences; and they could be vicious. Mercifully they only lasted about a year. These were essentially the troubled times.

Eamonn de Valera's father was a Spanish/American onion seller who married a girl from County Galway and deserted her in America when she was 'with child'. My grandfather raised the wherewithal to bring her back to Ireland and she was employed by the rector of Queenstown (now Cobh). The child was to become a giant of Ireland but not popular with the Royal Irish Constabulary. He was arrested several times and once when making a speech in Sligo. After release from prison he returned to Sligo, beginning his speech with 'as I was saying when I was so rudely interrupted . . .' Sligo, the county town, boasted a very honourable firm of solicitors named Messrs Argue and Phibbs!

These were anxious days for our parents. Children were being kidnapped – or so at least it was being rumoured – and I believe they felt it of God's mercy that my father was invited to become Vicar of St. John's Deptford, SE London.

Many memories remain from Ireland. Blissful holidays in Rathclaren Rectory, near Courtmachsherry; the finding of ambush trenches on the hill overlooking Western Avenue in Cork; and, above all, a Mission of Healing conducted by an Anglican clergyman named Hickson, when I received back my sight from a condition of crippling short-sightedness. This became a matter of wide and controversial interest in Cork but to me it was an occasion of knowing that God was real and that I now belonged to Him. Mr Hickson was a house guest and I had said I didn't want to be part of the Mission. I was self-conscious about my sight and the oculist, Mr Townsend of a prominent Cork family, had said I would be severely

restricted by it. I liked Mr Hickson and finally decided to seek
healing. I don't remember the order of service but I sat with
my mother and aunt in the north side aisle. The time came to
go forward to kneel at the Communion rails and I was given
a card to hold saying what my need was. Mr Hickson laid his
hands on my head and I imagined I was aware of a light about
me as he prayed a prayer I can't remember. 'Can you see?' was
the urgent question which met me on return to the pew. I said
'yes', I could not disappoint them! I was given a prayer book
and as I looked at what was all blurred I saw the letters take
shape. I *could* see! The short-sightedness had gone and years
afterwards when I was treated for astigmatism as an under-
graduate I told the eye specialist of my past experience. 'There
is not a scrap of short-sight in you now', he said.

Irish memories are still with me and they are of a gentle
people who had time for children. But there was poverty too.
Women wore shawls in all weathers and who could tell what
quality of ragged clothes their shawls covered. The children
were barefooted and eager for any coins they might gain.

I remember sitting in the large bay window above a shop
on the South Mall. There was a temporary platform erected
almost opposite the window and de Valera was to address a
huge crowd assembled . . . I was supplied with boiled sweets
as I watched the proceedings, but was not allowed to chew
them. Michael Collins was to have a similar hearing the next
week, but this was not quite without incident.

It was shortly after this that Michael Collins was murdered,
but the Republicans as distinct from the Free State took power
in December 1922.

I can still see the yard outside Cork railway station with

people coming out requiring transport. To do this they would hold up their arms above their heads. If they touched hands over their heads then up would drive a closed cab, if their hands were apart then their vehicle was the jaunting car, which was an open contraption with seats on each side back to back and with the 'jarvey' sitting high up on a box immediately forward of the seats.

The Royal Irish Constabulary was a fine and disciplined body of men of 'guardsman' stature. One evening we were seated round the fire in my father's study when he was out. Jane – our cook – was 'on duty' that night and she came in in great agitation. 'O Lor' Mum, there's an awful looking man in the doorway and he wants the master . . . now he says he wants you.' My mother went but to find a tall stranger muffled right up in dark coat and turned-up collar. 'Are you the Rector's wife?' he asked as he drew a revolver from his pocket. 'Yes', she said 'What do you want?' 'I'm a policeman in disguise' he said, 'The Chief Constable thought that you might all be safer if the rector had this.' My mother didn't trust herself to take it she just opened the cloakroom door and told him to put the revolver on the table.

One of my father's sisters, Aunt Bertha, came to stay with us after the 1914 – 1918 War. She had been a 'Fanny' driver in France and she was a great favourite with us boys. She was anxious to help the police in their 'law and order' role, but she would only do this on horseback. The Chief Constable consented to her being some sort of 'special' if she could control the most difficult horse they had in their stables. We admired her in her blue 'get up' as she patrolled in the city. She later married Jim Greated of Lydigin Castle in Galway and she arrived at the church on a jaunting car behind a drunken 'jarvey'. There was rioting on the streets and the rioters ceased their activities to cheer her, but the driver of the hired limousine had refused to risk the journey. Uncle Jim was a fine landlord but the locals demanded his land. He was rigidly strict about rents being paid but, if a cottager really could not pay his rent then Uncle Jim paid it for him and so kept his books straight. Due to the troubles the time came when they were locked in the stables and the castle (a small one) was burned to the ground. Years after, a local wept on his deathbed saying 'I wish to Gawd I'd never done that to Mister Jimmy'.

To leave Ireland was as sad as it was exciting. To go to live in London meant strange importance, but there were our friends to leave behind and they were there on St Patrick's Quay to see us off. We hoped we would sail on the Classic – the newer, more glamorous boat – but it was to be on the Glengarif and somehow this fitted the mood . . . we were missing something. Ireland has some quality about it – a mystic quality – it does not belong to you but you belong to it. In a strange way I still do.

Chapter II

MAKING OUR HOME IN ENGLAND

The move to London meant a completely new life for all of us. We travelled from Cork to Fishguard by boat taking our cook and, I think, two maids. It was a rough crossing when even the cat, which was in the cook's care, failed to keep her discomfort to herself.

A town house of some four storeys seemed bunched together and quite unlike home. The gas light was activated by heavy tumble switches which released the gas to be ignited by a small by-pass flame alongside the gas mantles. The telephone was different, for the Cork one (number Cork 28) had a handle which one 'rang' and a mouthpiece which attached to the box and an ear piece which one held to the ear. In the London house we had discovered speaking tubes to the kitchen from the first and second floors and we boys got tangled up between these and the local telephone exchange.

I think my parents expected that England would be more 'cultured' or perhaps formal than Ireland, but soon their instructions to be 'extra well behaved' with the families we would meet became instructions to be very choosy and often to stand apart from them. School and parish friends were regarded as 'not suitable' to invite to the house, and we felt under tension between loyalty to friends and loyalty to parents.

I was fortunate in my preparatory school about which the parents were totally relaxed. Belmont House was in Blackheath, was run by the Misses Barff and staffed by people of stature and culture. It was a 'bus ride to school each morning and, time permitting, I would 'miss' the first bus if it had solid rather than pneumatic tyres. All were 'open' on top and each seat had a canvas cover which could be hooked across to protect it, but not the occupant, from rain.

The protectiveness of our godly and loving parents was overwhelming. My eldest brother was not allowed to take up a scholarship he had won to Clifton College and for me the choice of school between Westminster, Dulwich and St Dunstan's was determined by my parents on the advice of a Bishop Howe, the then Bishop of Woolwich. We boys must live at home because English boarding schools might/ would endanger our moral standards. We three elder boys all became Dunstonians one by one, although Robin (the second son) was withdrawn for private tuition given by a certain Dr Weymouth. Before going to St. Dunstan's, where I was awarded a Foundation Scholarship, Robin and I had some very happy years at Belmont House prep school in Blackheath which served the Woolwich Garrison as well as such as us. Standards were high, Christian values were paramount and the teaching was good. I still have valued memories of the staff to whom I must have seemed a difficult and idle boy.

St Dunstan's was a different experience. It was a progressive competitive school under the able head-ship of the Revd. F G Forder who had recently assumed his appointment from that of being a Housemaster at Charterhouse. The assistant master I most admired was L F Morris who later wrote the history of the College and gave all his life and resources to its well-being. For me the tension of home loyalties was enormously strong. I was better at home than spending 'too much time at games'; dramatic art was not for a sensitive Christian boy (I was allowed once only to attend a school play, *The Tempest*) and OTC was permissible but not the possible corruption of OTC camp. I tried my best about this for without camp there was no promotion in the OTC and no prefect-ship in the school was open to any boy who was not an NCO in the OTC. Grudgingly it was agreed that if Bishop Taylor Smith recommended my going to camp when next he stayed with us then so be it. Bishop Taylor Smith came to stay and preach for my father and recommended camp – but I was not allowed to go. Forder gave me a reference I did not deserve – 'record in every way entirely satisfactory ... industrious and thoughtful and has the right outlook' etc, but my school record was undistinguished and I got a shocking report from my Housemaster who ran the OTC; he said I would never qualify for a commission in the Army. Was this my fault or my parents', or was it his inability to recognise the difficulties I faced in refusing to go to OTC camp. Certainly OTC camp was his criterion of judgement for all.

The tempo of life in those days was very different from today. Heavy traffic was restricted to 12 mph and cars to 20 mph. The Kingston by-pass had recently been built and Robin (my second brother) was stopped by the police for driving at 50 mph in our Morris Oxford – he asked the police if they would give him a certificate to prove the car had achieved 50 mph! In those days one was entitled to hold a driving licence without a driving test at the age of 15!

Times of tension there may have been but I can never thank God enough for my parents. Their encouragement in Christian things was enormous and their example challenging. Under the leadership of my eldest brother Theodore – known by most in later years as John – we young people formed ourselves into an active and purposeful Christian group named Missionary Union – I still have a silver tie pin bearing the Greek letter 'μ' which was our emblem. We ran open-air services, interested ourselves in missionary societies and generally headed up the young peoples' ministry in the parish. Girl friends were taboo and we had to handle this situation as best we could for the old 'not suitable' barriers were quite inflexible. Nevertheless, I still remember my father's advice that if I liked a girl I should look at her mother and her home for whoever I married would grow very much like her mother, and 'home' for me would be of the quality of her upbringing.

I left school as early as I was allowed. The tensions were uncomfortable and I knew what I thought I wanted to be – a medical missionary. The medical element was persuaded into me by my parents and I had accepted it. So it was that I went to St. Bartholomew's Hospital as a student at the age of sixteen and – up to a point – enjoyed it.

My father accepted another parish, that of St Andrew-the-Less in Cambridge. My eldest brother Theodore was already at Emmanuel College and Robin was struggling to achieve his 'Little-Go'. Here was my chance for Cambridge too for, based at home my parents could afford it – with some outside help – and besides 'it would never do for me to be left on my own in London!'

The idea appealed to me because an arts degree would help towards preparation for ultimate ordination. It meant, however, that I had to begin all over again. I had not done well in my School Certificate to the horror of the school – perhaps it was because I sat the examination papers with a high temperature. Because of this I had sat the College of Preceptors examination in the autumn and had passed it. But this was not enough for Cambridge and so I had to sit the Little-Go in order to matriculate. This was not difficult except that the set books in Latin and English were different from the set books of Oxford and Cambridge School Certificate and Lucretius was entirely new to me. I was now 19 years old.

Jesus College was generous enough to accept me and I remember how Canon Abbot and the Senior Tutor – 'Gus Elliot' – both seemed to care that I passed the College Entrance. I loved it there but I had lost my vision of medicine and actively disliked anatomy and its dissecting. Most afternoons had to be spent in the 'meaters', the anatomy school, and there was no time for sustained sport. I rowed in the rugger boat one year but preferred sculling which I could do as time allowed, and I played lacrosse because it did not demand the same time as other games. I never attained a half-blue but did on occasion play for the University. Squash and badminton both found a place in my time-table but I was still the same 'lone' boy which I had drifted into being at school.

Occasionally I took out a horse from the stables in Hobson Street. Old Mr Hobson was long dead, for otherwise I might have been given a winded nag. He chose the horse for its rider and there was no gain-saying – hence 'Hobson's choice'. That I was no fit rider is illustrated by an event not forgotten by my brothers. I was returning from 'The Gogs' when the horse was more anxious to get back to the stables than I was. He suddenly threw me and galloped away. I returned on foot to the stables – self-conscious in riding kit – to report 'loss of horse', but there was the horse looking at me over the door of the stable with a wicked gleam in his eye.

My degree was only a pass degree because of my dislike of medicine but I added psychology in which I did reasonably well and found fascinating, and I added church history in which I believe I 'surprised' Gardner-Smith, the Dean of Jesus, for I had done it in my own time. It was hearing Bryan Green conduct a mission to London University when I was at Barts which first interested me in psychology. He seemed to deal with people rather than with a subject although he obviously had a fine command of his subject.

While studying at Cambridge I had some sort of double life. Work and college activities constituted the greater demand but I found extra-mural time for Christian work. I got linked up with the Church at Dry Drayton and established a Sunday School for the village children. There were some twenty–twenty-five who crowded into the school-room on Sunday mornings and then would climb onto a bone-shaker while I drove them to the village Church. Occasionally I was trusted to preach. My sister Margaret (Bema her name within the family) travelled with me to play the piano and was a tower of strength. Ultimately I was summoned to the University Proctor's office – I was 'progged' because I was not allowed to run a car in term time. The proctor was more generous than I deserved and allowed me to purchase a university licence at half its cost. The car was a ten year old Austin 12hp tourer which I had bought for £2. Later I became more extravagant and bought a Talbot for £7, having sold my Austin to a breaking-up yard for £4.

Summer holidays, both before going up to Cambridge and while there, were spent doing Children's Special Service Mission work (CSSM) at Weymouth, Milford-on-Sea, and Bembridge. This occupied the month of August when, as member of a team and finally leading one, we invited children of public and private school background to attend informal beach services followed by sporting activities on both morning and afternoon. It was unforgivably 'selective', but was an attempt to share the love of God with young people who would not normally be reached by 'Sunday Schools'. Varsity students, young Naval and Army Officers and some older people ran these missions and there was no remuneration for anybody, everyone paid his or her own way. My days ended with the CSSM when the principal of my Theological College demanded my concentration on preparing for ordination. I was to have no distractions from the College, and I was not to take part in its outreach to local hospitals, etc.

A year at home after Cambridge (my father had moved to West Kensington) involved me in further Christian activity and in parish interests before I went to the London College of Divinity to prepare for ordination. It was a two-year course which I completed in four terms because of anxiety to get to grips with ministry. I did not recognise that this was sheer folly and impatience. How often I wished I had done the longer BD course instead of rushing through the General Ordination Examination.

I went to my father as curate. He had become heavily involved in clearing up a 'Trust' scandal. The Martyrs' Memorial Trust had been betrayed by an unworthy secretary and my father was faced with the re-organisation of this trust which sponsored some very famous public schools and which had the advowson (power to appoint) to some hundreds of parishes. This meant that his parish work was suffering and that he needed a curate who would understand the situation and accept its inequality of burden sharing. In addition to this I drove him round to visit parishes in the Gift of the Trust and really got to know him better. We had given up keeping a car because of garaging difficulties and we used the self-drive facilities of Daimler Hire. This was but £1 per day for a 16 hp Daimler or we could have a Lanchester for fifteen shillings or a straight 8 cylinder Daimler for twenty-five shillings. He was generosity personified, encouraging me and directing me without overmuch 'paternalism' and it was only when he moved parish on his accepting the rectorship of Tooting that our partnership ended. During this time I had been doing service with the Christian Evidence Society at Hyde Park Corner (tub thumping) and in some way was beginning to form a wider approach to evangelistic and pastoral work.

My association with the CSSM had meant friendship with many Naval and Military people. I worked at first under a World War I Colonel (ES Cooper) who was a friend of my parents' and was 'intercession secretary' of the Officers

Christian Union. Later, the Assistant Chaplain General of Eastern Command came to live in the parish and he used to play squash with me at the Hurlingham Club where he usually defeated me. Both Colonel Cooper and JH McKew (the Assistant Chaplain General) interested me – I think unintentionally – in applying for an Army ministry.

It was while curate to my father that I met Pat Bartholomew who was to become my wife. Her godmother was a parishioner and a friend; and Pat had just returned from a year in Ceylon spent with her father during his last year in Colonial Service there. It was suggested that we included her in a family party to the Keswick Convention in the Lake District and I returned from that week in Keswick with a certain gentleness of heart toward her. A year later, once again at Keswick, we became secretly engaged for I felt it wrong to tell anyone until I had her parents' approval. After all, she was in the care of my family. My parents – particularly my mother – expressed disappointment that I had not told them but I thought, and still think, I was right.

When my father left the parish of St Mary, West Kensington, I decided to stay on until the arrival of the new vicar. At this time Pat encouraged me towards the Army. Her family had strong Naval and Army connections and she and they became a very significant part of my decision to go and seek the advice of Mr McKew. He, too, was encouraging, and the Chaplain General (Thorold) received my application and called me for interview. 'I see,' he said, 'you have given Bishop Taylor Smith as a referee. How well do you know him?' I explained that I knew him as a friend of the family and I hoped he would recommend me despite his being abroad at that time. 'Do you know' went on Dr Thorold 'if Bishop Taylor Smith recommends you and I turn down your application it is as much as my job is worth?'

Joining the Chaplains' Department was not as easy as it promised to be. I had agreed to be available in the autumn of 1938 and not to contemplate marriage until I'd had six months to learn my job as a chaplain. The Munich Crisis, ending in what later proved to be only a temporary 'agreement' with Hitler, brewed up and the posting for which I was earmarked was no longer a possibility so my appointment to an Army Chaplaincy was deferred. I had been designated as Chaplain to a new Army Technical Engineering School which would have been opened at Chatham had it not been that the Munich Crisis had upset and delayed these plans. I wrote to the Chaplain General saying that I proposed to take another appointment in the home church, that I would marry now and not wait, and, with his agreement, apply to him again in two or three years time.

Pat and I were married by my father, assisted by my brother Robin who had by now been ordained some two years, at Pat's parish church in Outwood, Surrey (17 September 1939) and I never cease to thank God for the 57 years we had together.

In those days one was very much left to one's own discretion in regard to one's career. I was offered the Parish of Aspinall, near Ware in Hertfordshire, thanks to my father's influence, and Pat and I went up to see the church wardens and to see the very lovely country church and its dream rectory. Dr Freer, the Bishop of St Albans, wrote to me inviting me to see him and, on the morning of my going to St

Albans I got a letter from my own bishop (Winnington-Ingram) saying he was surprised to know I was visiting his brother bishop at St Albans without his knowledge. By now I was beginning to feel that I was too young and too inexperienced to become the rector of however small a parish. Bishop Freer knew that I was emphatically Low Church and he was known as an equally emphatic Anglo-Catholic! He received me very kindly but said 'Everything you have heard of me is dirt, so I am not going to advise you'. We talked for a while until I asked if I might have his advice. He said 'Don't touch it with a barge-pole, it will be the end of your ministry and you'll end up maintaining a lovely garden and digging potatoes.' I had written a letter of apology to Bishop Winnington-Ingram saying that I would make no decisions without reference to him, so I went to see him in double-quick time by appointment. He could not have been more kind. I was right, he told me, in not accepting the parish and 'would I trust him to select a second curacy for me?' He sent me to Barham Gould whose ministry at St Paul's, Onslow Square in Kensington was very alive but, unfortunately for me, only that morning Barham Gould had given the appointment to another man.

I went off the same day to see if Bryan Green had a vacancy at Crouch End. Bryan Green was about to go to Holy Trinity Brompton but welcomed me as a junior curate and took me temporarily to Brompton with him for a matter of a few weeks. Then I was to return to Crouch End and await the appointment and arrival of the new vicar, Frank Chadwick, afterwards Bishop of Barking. Frank was a challenging influence in my life and ministry, but only for a very short time.

Just before he arrived I was summoned to the War Office, told that the appointment/posting might now be a possibility and that I should re-apply forthwith, or perhaps not at all.

The Churchwardens, Bishop Vernon of Willesden and Frank Chadwick all were as kind as they were understanding and it was agreed that I would remain in the parish under Frank Chadwick for a short few months before my acceptance of the Army Chaplaincy after Easter 1939.

Chapter III

AN ARMY CHAPLAIN

Life in the Army was something entirely new. Later I used to say that the raw recruit after he had been give a number, had had a haircut, and had lost his civilian mode of dress was in a whirl of disorientation. Ranked as a Captain I felt as raw as any recruit. I tried to salute the Regimental Sergeant Major – but he got up first. My cap blew off my head as I was driving past the sentry and receiving his salute at Brompton Barracks in Chatham – I'm sure he was amused! But kindness, tolerance and welcome surrounded me. My Senior Chaplain – RJ Stockdale – left the nitty gritty of advice to TEG Morris who was a chaplain under him but senior to me in service. Tommy Morris took me to call on the General Officer Commanding and astonished me by saying, as we mounted the stairs, 'Put your gloves on'. 'Yes, but why?' I asked. 'In uniform you shake hands in gloves.' My Senior Chaplain took me to meet and pay my respects to the Commandant of the ATS as the 'Apprentice Tradesmen's School' was designated before women donned uniform in the Army. Lt.Colonel 'Dan' Perrott who was to be my immediate commanding officer looked at me solemnly across his table, 'We've met before' he said. About a year or two before we had been introduced to one another at a garden party in Wimbledon by an elderly friend who had forgotten both our names and had to ask us each in turn.

No one could have had a better introduction to the Army. It was early in my Service, when I was on duty on my own at the Garrison Church in Chatham, that the vestry door opened and the Commandant of the School of Military Engineering said 'Padre, you're all on your own. Can I help?' He read the lessons as I have seldom heard them read. Years later he was Chief Engineer of the Army and I was proud to know General Pat Campbell (Sir Douglas) as a senior friend. The Apprentice Boys' Camp was an absorbing job. 'Learn the list of the boys' names before the draft arrives' my senior chaplain advised. This was to help to identify and to get to know the boys, all about 15 years old. They were a splendid lot of well-recruited eager boys who as yet knew little discipline, and I had them for morning prayers as a parade each morning at 7.45 AM, also for Religious Instruction during their working programme and for Sunday Parade services. Confirmation classes and all such opportunities were in 'spare time' but every assistance was given. Each morning, together with the Company Commanders, I attended the Commandant's briefing and was made to feel an essential part of the establishment. Colonel Dan Perrot was a man of immense 'presence' and deep Christian faith who had the gift of bringing the best out of the men he commanded whatever their rank and expertise. His serious demeanour added an extra quality to a dry sense of humour, and his loss of life

later in or around Tobruk – reported missing' – was a real loss
to the Army.

The only 'Sports Day' for which I was to be at Chatham will
live for ever in my memory. This was the first 'Open Day' to
the parents of the boys, and they would see their young 'smart
as smart could be' on uniformed parade and in recreational
sports. Excitement was high and anticipation eager. But the
day started wet and threatening. The weather report was foul
and I found my Morning Prayers assembly depressed and
thoroughly down. Earlier – as Pat and I were praying together
before the days work – she had said to me 'You must pray with
the boys about the weather'. I entered the East Dining Hall
saying in my heart 'Lord, if you don't answer – I've "had it"'.
We read the story of the stilling of the storm on the Lake of
Galilee and I asked the boys if any had ever felt they'd had a
prayer answered would they raise their arms. Many did so.
'Right, we're going to ask God about the weather.' 'Nice
answer to our prayers, Padre' was being said to me in sunshine by 11.0 AM. But at 2.30, waiting for the parade to march
on, the heavens blackened and a threatening heavy drop or
two saw the donning of mackintoshes. The clouds, which
sometimes seem to converge over Chatham, met. They rolled
to either side of the camp spilling their contents – but the camp
was dry. 'If anyone wants to know the reason for the extraordinary behaviour of the weather' said the Commandant at
Prize-Giving 'let them ask any boy who attended the 7.45 am
parade in the East Dining Hall this morning.'

Meanwhile clouds of another sort were rolling up which
were not to spare us. Obviously war was imminent and anxiety
mounted day by day. I was conducting the Sunday Parade

Service when a note was passed to me saying that war had been declared. Rightly or not, I did not disclose the news until we got to that part of the service given to intercessory prayers and, before the service had ended, we found ourselves in the air-raid shelters awaiting an air attack. It was a false alarm.

A day or two later I received my orders to report to 9th Infantry Brigade in 3rd Division at Portsmouth. My senior chaplain saw me off in the early hours of the following morning and took my wife back with him to breakfast with his wife. They sang the praises of chaplains in action and claimed – correctly – that a higher proportion of chaplains had given their lives in the first world war than any other regiment had. This was not wholly a comforting thought for a young wife perplexed by all that lay before her.

Already with the Royal Engineers at Chatham I had seen the Sappers in Brompton Barracks being issued with their arms and I, too, was issued with 'camp kit' as were all officers. Chaplains are not issued with hand-guns – they neither carry nor use weapons. Thus equipped and carrying a most unwieldy valise, I was staggering through Portsmouth when I met a kindly but very 'alive' officer who asked my destina-tion and sent greetings to Brigadier Robb, my Brigade Commander. This officer said that he was the Divisional Commander but in my ignorance I carried his greeting as from 'The Commander in Chief'. But Monty – for it was he, was in due course to fulfil an ignorant prophecy becoming Field Marshal Viscount Montgomery of Alamein.

The Brigade was moving to Dorset and I was invited just to keep in touch for a few days and to be available for moving as required. An aunt of my wife's – Mrs Bernard Curry – and a naval widow offered me hospitality. She was the Hon. Lady Superintendent of the Royal Sailors' Rest (Aggie Westons) and so I saw a little of the sailors adjusting to what was to be their gallant and often grim task.

We, as a brigade HQ, moved into Wraxall Manor, a little distance from Dorchester, and Pat was welcomed as a paying guest in the retired home of a clergy widow in Rampisham near by. My chaplaincy duties were to cover 2nd RUR, the Church of England element of the KOSB, the 253 Field Company of the Royal Engineers and the 9th Field Ambulance. A lot of time, therefore, was spent on the road for it was decided that I should live in at Brigade Headquarters.

· It was after dinner one night that the brigadier asked me to wait to have a talk. How long had I been in the Army? What experience of service life had I had? And then, with the greatest kindness he advised me what to expect and how to deal with complainers who would take advantage of a young and green padre. But, he said, if the men stop complaining 'come to see me at once' for something serious may well be wrong.

Some days later lunch was disturbed by urgent confidential messages being brought to Jumbo Leicester the Brigade Major (a Marine who later commanded the Marine Commandos, or Green Berets). It became a hurried lunch and soon we were on informal parade outside, duly hatted and gloved. The car that stopped beside us was flying the Royal Ensign and it was King George VI himself who got out and shook us each by the hand. – I hurried away afterwards to shake my wife's hand with the same glove!

We sailed from Southampton to Cherbourg on a very uncomfortable sea and – advised by a senior RAF chaplain on

board – I went round finding volunteers for a ship's concert at
the foot of the main gangway. We all cheered each other up by
singing 'We're here because we're here because' . . . and I discovered my batman driver had an excellent singing voice and
quite a good repertoire. His favourite song then was 'Trees'.
At least I had a bunk overnight but not so the unfortunate soldiery who lay anywhere in corridors, etc.

The gentleness of what some would mistakenly have called
the rough and rude soldiery again and again disclosed itself.
Before embarking for France we had had an exercise in the
rough and each of us was allowed the very minimum
bedding. I was lying – and trying to gain some sleep and mis-
erably cold – when someone threw an extra blanket over me.
It proved to be the Mess Orderly (a reservist who looked after
dykes in East Anglia). It was his blanket and he had just got
up for early Mess Duty and thought I looked cold.

Moving off from Cherbourg, we stopped first in the
Chateau at Sille le Guillaum near Etienne where the owner
made everything available to us. My duty of censoring letters
had already begun and I was intrigued to read how shocked
soldiers were to find the 'grand houses' were horribly
draughty and far short of even the little luxuries of comfort
and warmth they had enjoyed at home.

Finally we reached Templemars near Lille and settled in
gradually as the 'phoney war' disclosed itself. My time was
spent visiting the units assigned to me and getting to know
officers and men. NAAFI had not yet come 'forward' and
indeed never came forward beyond Divisional Headquarters
at Seclin. Within the first few weeks I took over a lock-up
garage and began buying – first from down the line at

railhead, and then at Seclin – the cases of chocolate, cigarettes, razor blades, etc. which were in unceasing demand. Here one got to know many people who would stop for a chat and frequently open their hearts. I had regular hours of canteen opening and – with no complaints to me – never opened on a Sunday.

Page, my batman/driver, who was not yet a committed Christian, was a splendid helper. In the pub/estaminet across the road he encountered a number of soldiers who entered into religious argument with him because he looked after 'the Padre'. This led to some coming to see and talk with me for themselves. LF Page was a joy to have with his Lancashire wit and faithful loyalty right up to the time when I became a senior chaplain in Aldershot.

Sometimes one met with most unexpected rewards. I had taken a nucleus of our brigade concert party to 8th Brigade sappers fairly near-by and this nucleus had awakened the entertaining skills in 8th Brigade. The evening was over and I was about to close down when up jumped a not over-articulate sapper not only to say 'thank you' but to say that Padre did more than run concerts and that he held many informal services, etc, that he cared about people's real selves and the evening should not be allowed to end without asking the Padre to pray for us all.

One day in the Mess before lunch I was idly knocking a few billiard balls around on one of those strange continental tables that have no pockets. In walked a visitor who asked what on earth that table was all about. He was the Duke of Gloucester who was expected to lunch (not quite so informally) and I taught him one or two of the nonsense tricks of the table. He remembered this when – years after – I met him when I was preaching at the Royal Chapel in Windsor!

The phoney war provided a degree of excitement when occasional reconnaissance planes flew overhead searching out our Brigade task of extending the Maginot Line. The Maginot Line had been built as a supposedly secure defence barrier between France and Germany and the first task of the newly arrived British Forces was to extend the line northwards. Digging was the order of the day as well as intensive and hard training. Contrary to what the history of the 3rd Division says it was our Transport Corporal – Corporal Guttridge – who was to become Monty's driver – who devised the idea of a hidden illuminated white patch on our vehicles' differential boxes and who thereby enabled us to move at night safely and, apparently, without lights. This puzzled the Germans during our later retreat to Dunkirk.

Of course the phoney war could not last. Lord 'Haw Haw's nightly after dinner entertainment attempting to undermine British morale, usually followed the chimes of Big Ben, with his opening and drawling words – 'The death knell of the British Empire' – was growing thin and neither side was suing for peace 'at any price'. Lord 'Haw Haw' was of Irish descent and had been known as an agitator, a street politician in Dulwich in South East London. He had the most appalling affected accent. Rumours were building up and 'leave' at home – which had been promised by Monty as a possibility – was cancelled just as it was about to begin. For my part, it was obvious that, if battle joined, I should attach myself to a battalion and not live at Brigade Headquarters. Accepted by the RUR I prepared to move to them – and only just in time.

Chapter IV

TO DUNKIRK

We moved forward into Belgium in well ordered convoy for our training had been excellent. There was something almost sinister in the air due to civilians en route wanting to sell us postcards and claiming to know where we were going and then being at our secret destination again selling postcards. A strange vehicle joined the convoy at one stage, two vehicles in front of me, and began queue hopping. It has no identification numbers such as we had telling the initiated to what Division, Brigade or Battalion HQ it belonged. As dawn came we were strafed by an enemy fighter plane and my driver/batman (Page, a reservist of the Kings Own) was out on the road in an instant training his rifle on the plane. Mathematicians had worked out that an aircraft strafing on the dive would deliver a bullet every eight feet . . . but neither man nor vehicle was hit.

We bivouacked on the hills outside Louvain, our forward convoys moving into the city and taking up positions along the railway line. Despatch riders provided the links between the companies and Battalion HQ, and our dispatch riders, 'Don Rs' as they were called, proved unsung heroes. They rode through enemy fire, threatened by snipers and hidden hazards in pursuit of their essential work. Enemy it was by now. 'Jerry' has ceased just to be 'Jerry' for he was now a threat. We were attacked the first night by bombs which screeched as they came down and crumped around us. It was the first time I felt the loneliness of being under fire and 'keeping my head down' as discipline required. At first light I climbed out of my shallow trench and went round fearing many casualties. No one had been hurt but it was decided we would be better placed right in the centre of Louvain rather than on its outskirts.

Two junior officers were sent off to reconnoitre a place and the Battalion HQ followed to find out that they were to be stationed in one of Lille's better restaurants which had a good cellar and was surrounded by plate glass. Lt.Col Fergus Knox – our outstanding CO – allowed me to complain and gave me ten minutes to find a better alternative. The Regimental Aid Post then was part of Battalion HQ and plate glass was no happy housing for casualties in transit. Across the Grand Place and with its main door unlocked stood the Town Hall with its excellent position and massive walls. We settled for that. Mortar bombs fell harmlessly about us – for, of course, the enemy knew where we were – and we went back across the road to feed as occasion allowed.

My first real baptism of fire was when I went forward with the second in command to see the forward troops in their improvised positions. Our gunner support was pouring fire down on the enemy lines only a few yards distant and we felt that if we stood upright then we would be casualties to our own guns! It took a little time to realise that the whistling bullet and whining shell were a safe distance away. The near-miss made a crack like a very close rifle shot and the flight of the close shell would not have been heard at all by any casualty. This I learned for myself, in taking a funeral of a rifleman in 'A' Company, while climbing over a high wall in the station yard. The really forward companies finally were completely pinned down and cut off and I shall always remember the solid courage and fine leadership of 'Slappy Reid', the company commander.

'Sir, I have to report the loss of one of our anti tank guns' reported the young officer in command of these, our two-pounder anti-tank guns. The enemy had cut his gun off with intensive gun fire but had not yet collected it. 'What do you mean? Lost? You know where it is! Go and get it.' Such was discipline and not without the concern of the CO. Without complaint the YO returned to risk his life and retrieve his gun under enemy fire.

Then came the unbelievable news. The Maginot Line had been breached on its northern extremity. 'They shall not pass' proved empty words and we were now cut off. Belgian troops gave the impression of undisciplined flight and we were instructed to move back to Brussels to 'prepared positions' – a designated area would have been a better description! Our Belgian liaison officer burnt the Union Jack openly in the 'Grand Place' as we were preparing to leave Louvain. He maintained that if it was lost it would fall into enemy hands, but certain of the riflemen were very disturbed and suspicious. They suspected it was a signal to the enemy, and they regarded that flag almost as equating to a regimental Colour.

Those of us with vehicles were driven back to the 'prepared position' overlooking Brussels but the majority of the Battalion had to march all twenty or so miles. Never would one have thought that men could sleep as they marched, but many maintained that they had. The Louvain experience had been exhausting – for active service respects no observance of working hours. How weary one could be was evidenced by a YO who gave his report in Louvain to his CO, turned and saluted in the doorway, and immediately fell asleep propped against the door post.

From the hills above Brussels we watched a small number of enemy planes bomb the city but we could not tell whether they were attacking selected targets or bombing at random – it was not very effective. Withdrawal was the order as far as we were concerned. Gradually, and finally with increasing certainty, we knew we were heading towards the coast. The enemy tanks were everywhere wreaking havoc in our lines of communication. As we got near the Lille/Roubaix area we heard that NAAFI had deserted their main supply depot. No food rations had been reaching us. 'Communications' scarcely existed and we were living off the land. The CO readily granted me permission to take a 30cwt truck back to Roubaix and collect what I could from the deserted NAAFI stores. On arrival at first light I discovered that other people, too, had had the same idea! We found tinned food and – to the disappointment of some – I used the major half of the truck for this, but there was still enough room for chocolates, cigarettes, beer and spirits to cheer many hearts.

The supporting Gunners were reduced to minimal

ammunition and their response to our requests for covering fire became 'Will you have it now, or will you wait for emergency?' Wherever we went there were the same 'civilians' selling rubbish cards etc. and evidence abounded of our positions being made known to the enemy. Even gramophone records were found laid out in arrow formation to identify Battalion HQ.

At the very end when we were holding the perimeter around La Pannes/Dunkirk an RUR officer heard a soldier's call 'Coldstream Guards, Sir?' – 'No, Ulster Rifles' – 'Permission to fall out, Sir?' – 'Permission granted!' – and on investigation it was found that the wounded guardsman was already dead.

The final days seemed unreal. We had to dump our kit and destroy our vehicles without use of fire lest we disclosed our intentions. Water and oil were let out of the radiators and sumps of all vehicles and the engines were allowed to run at high speed until they seized up. As for ourselves, we retained personal arms where applicable, many officers changed into their best uniforms, breeches and field boots. As for me I wore my Service Dress, Sam Browne and breeches and only carried my Bible, my HC set and toilet equipment. My eldest brother, who had given me a pair of especially good boots, says that I returned with these slung round my neck! Perhaps I did, but I have no recollection of this. I know I carried my Bible, my Communion Set and my prayer book.

Pat could hear the noise of battle even in England and this was no comfort to her.

Colonel Dan Perrott – who had been my commandant in Chatham – was prominent in the ordering of the withdrawal procedures; it was he who devised the scheme of temporary 'piers' stretching out into the water and facilitating the embarkation of retreating troops. Lorries were driven as far out in the sea as possible and lashed end to end, boarding was lashed to the canopy frames and each person as he embarked was required to carry a sand bag and to drop it into the body of one of the lorries thereby giving it added stability. Our Royal Engineers Company Commander (Sir Charles Henneker) was hailed by Dan Perrott as he marched his company along the foreshore 'Honker, come here lad, I shoot plenty ammunition but I don't hit much'. Colonel Perrott was sitting in a deck chair, a smoking bren gun in one hand and a steaming mug of tea in the other! A lesser man might well have 'taken cover'. Years later his daughter, Helen, gave me a copy of the cryptic Army Order he had received directing him to prepare for and assume his duties on the beaches.

We approached the beach at its northern end in small parties – usually one officer with each, and walked towards Dunkirk via Bray Dunes along the foreshore. Above high water mark casualties of bombing and shelling lay unavoidably unburied. My group or party took advantage of low water and darkness on the last full day of evacuation. The sand was moist, but hard, and each of us left fluorescent footmarks as we walked along. The bombing had been stilled since nightfall and, mercifully, the enemy had not correlated his range of fire with the rise and fall of the tide. Shells fell in the soft sand reasonably well to our left.

Major Sir Charles Henniker who commanded the 253 Field Coy RE had had to lead his company in an infantry role holding back the enemy where a gap in our line of defence had occurred and his courage and leadership were proverbial. He had gathered his company when all thought they were cut off and said 'I don't know how many of you believe in prayer. I do. My advice to you now is "Pray as you've never prayed in your lives before. Don't pray to get home safely, but pray to have the guts to go through to the end whatever the end may be".'

The 253 Coy RE was a Territorial Company as distinct from a Regular Army Company of Engineers and I shall always remember one of their sergeants named Wingfield. During the days of withdrawal and when they were cut off from their command, Sgt. Wingfield had become both sergeant in command and a sort of father figure. 'Say a prayer' his men asked him one night, but he told me all he could do was to remember a line or two of Psalm 23 – The Lord is my Shepherd. The next night some of the men were able to add a few more words, and the third night even more. 'I never felt God's hand on my shoulder as I felt it then' he told me afterwards, and he added 'I'd go through the hell of Dunkirk again if only I could feel His hand again.' It was some months later that he wrote to tell me how real God had become to him at last.

Small boats were coming inshore and all ranks were making their way to and along the improvised piers. This was the first time it occurred to us that we might reach home safely. We were pulled off these jetties on to the small craft and taken off to the nearest ship.

The calm and purposeful firmness of all on destroyer *HM Vivacious* was almost as good as ultimately landing in Dover. They were totally exhausted plying to and fro between Dover and the beaches non-stop. They had lost their degussing (anti mine) protection through enemy action, but they were unperturbed. One soldier had been killed on board just before they picked us up and they said 'You chaps have been through it; it should have been one of us'. I found No.1 was burning his fingers with a lighted cigarette to keep himself awake.

We went on to Dunkirk off shore to try to collect others and there we were dive bombed. All my schoolboy love of Henty burst into reality as I heard the commands passing along the port and starboard decks, and then the guns! I've been knocked into the ditch by the dreaded German self-propelled, I've been too near the firing end of our own guns firing overhead and felt their blast, but nothing seemed to equal the *Vivacious'* roar of fury at those planes which failed to gain their target.

It was broad daylight as we zigzagged across the channel. The ship moved off with the thrust of a sports car as it left Dunkirk and we only 'heaved to' when the kindly sailors allowed me to bury at sea in a sail cloth the soldier whose death we all deeply regretted. He represented to us the loss of comrades and friends during the past grim days.

Chapter V
NORTHERN CLIMES

The white cliffs of Dover had a special significance as we steamed under their shelter at midday on 1 June 1940. Women Voluntary Service ladies were ashore to welcome us and to present each of us with some welcome fruit as a gift from Lord Nuffield, and trains were waiting to take us . . . no one knew where! Having 'identified' my train I made for the station telegraph office to send a telegram to Pat to say I was safely home. 'A greetings telegram?' was an inspired question from the person behind the counter.

We trundled off in the train hearing first that we were detraining at Aldershot, then somewhere on Salisbury Plain and finally as night approach we heard we were making for Porthcawl! Wales never seemed further away.

Hoteliers really welcomed us in the small hours of the morning, and comfortable rooms were allocated. No difficulties would be raised if wives could join us and so I telephoned Pat late as the hour was (about 4 am) and we were reunited that Sunday evening; A complete stranger drove me to

Bridgend to meet her train and this despite his petrol ration-
ing. In her railway carriage she found an old school friend
from prep school days who proved to be the wife of Arthur
Davies, one of the RUR Company Commanders!

When we surfaced on Sunday morning, after the first
luxury of sheets since battle had joined, we were told that
Porthcawl's barbers had opened their shops and would tidy
us up free of charge. Some of the banks, too, opened and
reached out to our financial needs despite our being without
chequebooks. Men's shops were ready to help with basic
clothing and, altogether, we were deeply moved by people's
welcoming generosity.

There was some confusion – certainly in my case – about
reporting home from the BEF. The local TA HQ registered us
in but, possibly did not know whom to inform about a chaplain! I was on the temporary missing persons' list for some
days at War Office. On the Sunday following I made myself
known to the Assistant Chaplain General of Western
Command (Barty Hughes) who was visiting the area, and
he told me to go home on immediate leave and await instruction.

The 3rd Division, including, of course, my Brigade, was
being re-equipped to return to France and it was only a matter
of days before a telegram arrived telling me to report to Frome
for re-attachment to my Brigade and Regiment. It seemed I
was only decently in time, for the advance vehicles were
being loaded up and were due to move off to the point of
embarkation at first light – but – and it was with very mixed
feelings, we heard that France had capitulated.

We became the much publicised 'Ironsides' force which

was rushed from one place to another awaiting the enemy's follow-through invasion. Lt.Col Brian Horrocks (of later very senior fame) told his class at the Staff College at that time that if the Germans were tempted to move on to Paris and so to achieve the goal they had failed to achieve in World War 1, then Britain had a chance; otherwise the situation was hopeless.

Morale was high not only with the soldiery but with the Home Guard who showed a gallant determination to defend their country to the last ditch. The RUR at one time found themselves based at Brighton (which, strangely, seemed later to have lost a number of its deck chairs), then at Corfe near Taunton, then in Thornbury Castle near Bristol, then in Beaminster in Dorset and a host of other places. While in Somerset a reputed encounter with a Home Guard countryman told of his halting a vehicle for identification purposes. 'Halt' the vehicle halted and the driver lowered the window of his car door. The Home Guard worthy moved forward and poked his rifle through the open window 'Halt!' he shouted again. The driver, edging his face away from the ugly weapon said 'But I have halted'. 'My order be to say "Halt" three times then fire!'

I was deeply hurt when we were billeted in Lancing College near Brighton and the bursar refused us the use of the chapel for our services. He said that soldiers' boots might cause damage to what I then rudely called his museum. We worshipped in one of Lancing's large form rooms, but with a sense of rejection by the school. I truly believe that the bursar's rejection would not have been upheld by the Governors.

Wives were officially 'not allowed' to join us, since the Division was highly operational, but many of us were able to find accommodation for our wives who had some petrol saved up for emergency, and we planned arrangements for their quick withdrawal if invasion proved imminent. In those days no officer was entitled to marriage allowance or any recognition of his marriage if he was under thirty years of age.

My senior chaplain asked me what I was going to do about Pat when Monty's firm order came out saying 'No wives to be in the neighbourhood'. I replied that I was not married! I was still under thirty and the Army did not recognise my married status! Pat remained discreetly with me!

Those were hectic days of movement and uncertainty, but days that could not long continue. Invasion had not come and the defensive thinking which it occasioned was becoming increasingly irrelevant. Counter invasion training now 'took over'. The Battle of Britain had been to many as much an experience of Divine providence as had been the withdrawal through Dunkirk, but our resources had been strained to the limit in terms of military equipment and aeroplanes. Life had to continue with church bells muted, road signs removed and anticipation of gloom. Marshall Aid was round the corner as our American friends realised that we were battered but not defeated and that they now had an unique opportunity to increase their influence and power in Europe. Isolation was still their national policy: yet they would support Britain to fight the Nazi peril to the last Englishman. They knew we would incur an ever increasing financial and moral debt to the States – their hope seemed to be that a European war would not have to involve them. Pearl Harbour changed all that. The world had gone mad with so many nations grasping oppor-tunities to increase wealth and power – and it was time for America to bestir itself.

The invasion barges and other shipping along the Pas de Calais no longer seemed to constitute a threat to us. Germany would now bomb us into submission and lay waste our country. They would reduce us to starvation and prevent our build-up of arms. Indeed, what they had failed to do with their armies they would seek to do by war on sea and in the air and by cutting off our communications with our Empire and with the US. No one was safe on the waters be he civilian or military and the Royal Navy accepted its protective and aggressive role with stupendous gallantry, and none can speak too highly of our airmen.

It was while 3rd Division was stationed at Blandford that – as the senior of the three chaplains in 9th Brigade – I was required to move to Divisional HQs in the absence of its senior chaplain. GW Younge, who had been our SCF (Senior Chaplain to the Forces) since our return to UK, was posted as SCF 18th Division bound for Singapore which was very soon overcome by the Japanese and Wilfrid Younge became a pris-oner of war in Changi. A new senior chaplain had to be appointed in 3rd Division and my role was that of acting SCF and answerable to the Deputy Assistant Chaplain General of the Corps.

A call from the War Office put a stop to my temporary responsibility and I found myself selected – as still a junior 'regular' chaplain – to accept the care of serving personnel on Flotta in the centre of the Orkney and Shetland defences. There had been complaints about the chaplain on Flotta. He

was really a little elderly for so exposed a posting, where cor-
rugated iron could be blown about like confetti in the wild-
ness of stormy weather, and military huts had to be wired
down against their being blown apart.

My accommodation was a section of a Jane hut, a WW1
wooden army hut set just behind the over-crowded Officers'
Mess. It was the only way I could have privacy and it was furnished with an iron bedstead, wire hooks for clothing, a rough
door placed on two trestles for a table, a folding chair, a croc-
odile stove, coal hod and poker! My first night was windy and
I could not use the table to write a note to Pat – everything was
rocking. I sat on the floor and wrote saying how glad I was
that the hut was wired down. In the morning I discovered my
hut was *not* wired down!

Flotta was the recreation island for the Fleet when the
weather was kindly, for it lay central to all the anchorages of
our ships. Battleships, aircraft carriers, cruisers and destroy-
ers made a magnificent show as they set out or returned from
Atlantic or North Sea convoy duties. I was told to expect temporary promotion as SCF of the Southern Isles in due time . . .
but due time was protracted and I was too busy to care.

I found about 2,000 men on an island so exposed that even
the cabbages had to be netted down and where no trees could
grow. Not even hedges were to be found but, instead, the
cattle were tethered.

We were in a prohibited zone and communications were
such that mail took a week to travel either way. Coastal
Defence Gunners were mostly northern men although I did
discover one man whom I had encountered when, as a young
curate, I had conducted funerals in Hammersmith Cemetery!

Heavy anti-aircraft gunners were Welshmen and the Light AA were survivors from the Coventry blitz. Sappers, REME and Pioneers were of mixed background and all were desperately lonely. The anti-aircraft guns were on immediate manning and this meant that men could never be away from their guns apart from a very small rota released on certain evenings to see a cinema show.

Always there was the pressure of high operational activity but in the Orkneys there was also much 'waiting about' in readiness for an enemy action which could occur without any warning. The sinking of *The Royal Oak* was an illustration of this. Radar was as yet generally unknown although one very secret site was concerned in this secret plotting of aerial traffic. The only occasion when I saw this at work was when I was shown a 'dot' which was an aircraft which appeared to be off any regular track and which disappeared as we watched its irregular progress. Tragically, this was almost certainly the aircraft in which the Duke of Kent lost his life.

A new senior chaplain arrived and in due course summoned us all to a conference at 11 AM in Kirkwall. Those of us from the smaller islands arrived late and received a sound reprimand. Drifters delayed by rough waters were no excuse for lateness! Very soon he was on his rounds visiting us and those with whom we worked. He happened to be on the same drifter with Lady Marjorie Dalrymple, a charming voluntary welfare officer, and she told me he had stood forward in the bow of the drifter taking the tossing in his stride, but she didn't tell me that on arrival on terra firma he had been as sick as a dog. He now knew the difficulties of the sea and how the drifters were quite unable to sail to time and, splendid person that he was, he issued an order tantamount to a genuine apology for his attitude to us at his conference.

But to return to one's work as a chaplain. I found in the loneliness and exposure of the island sites opportunity for closer touch with the men than was possible in the normal busy activity of service. Evening prayer services on the gun sites was genuinely treasured by them and we would brew up tea afterwards if the site happened to be the last visited that night. Each week I would visit each AA site during daylight and again for evening prayers, three or four sites each evening and, of course, there was the visiting of the larger units going on all the time, the hospital, and the seeing of men under discipline and confined to the guard room. Sunday was a mad rush from battery to battery and I think my Sunday record was thirteen services in one day. This included late evening prayers and informal sermon in one of the two Church of Scotland canteens on the island.

There were RAF balloon barrage sites also on the island and the airmen were really the chaplaincy charges of a visiting RAF chaplain. We called them the 'balloonatics'. One night a storm blew all but one balloon out to sea. Finally this balloon, being anchored to a three-ton lorry which was moored to the ground, made off with the lorry, carrying it over the cliffs and finally dumping it in the water! Some balloons got to Sweden and damaged their telephone and power lines with their trailing wires.

Once, when weather promised to be fair, I dared to organise Regimental Mock Sports after careful liaison with the units concerned. Admiral Tovey came ashore from the *King George V* battleship and Colonel Clayton Royal Marines made the bands of three battleships available. This was, I think, the only time the island had a half-day off and, I think, it did us all a lot of good. The PT sergeants were most intrigued with the crazy events I laid on. These latter I had learnt in Childrens' Special Services Missions in which I had been involved in student days.

We saw the American fleet sail in as the States became active in the war effort – the *Washington*, the *Tuskalousa* and the aircraft carrier *Wasp* made a noble sight as they cast anchor near those of our own battleships, carriers, county class and city class cruisers which were anchored in the Flow.

The enthusiastic interest of the American personnel in our defences did our people a lot of good and enlivened what was too often dull procedure. They were fascinated by our radar skills, until then unknown to them, and they tried unsuccessfully again and again to fly through our network. We were, at all levels, welcomed aboard their ships and, the Americans being inveterate souvenir hunters, sometimes our men would return ashore with their brass buttons missing from the back straps of their great coats. Standing one day behind the gun mechanism of a forward turret on the *Tuskalousa* I asked 'what would happen if I pressed this button?' I had trained the gun on, I think, the *Washington* and I was assured that the *Washington* would get very, very wet.

My great personal delight at this time was to have Pat with me. We lived in one room of a small farm cottage where we slept, cooked and entertained. It was all as primitive as it was fun, for there was no electricity or gas but a Tilley lamp for light and a small duck oven balanced on a Valor oil stove for cooking and there was an open fire. I had permission for her

to come up on a short term visit following surgery and a bout
of ill health. She at once offered help in serving teas etc in the
Church of Scotland canteen, which itself served Navy, Army
and RAF personnel and it seemed that her short stay in Flotta
was not to be 'too short'. The Naval Commander on the island
asked if she would be willing to give voluntary service at
Lyness, the main naval base, by working in the 'Confidential
Books' department. Thus it was that she anticipated the
WRNS in Orkney and was granted honorary officer status.
Each morning the Naval post wagon would stop on the road
near our cottage and drive her to the quay to embark for
Lyness. She became 'Our Lady' to some of the drifters which
acted as ferries and she was returned to Flotta each day, often
in time to accompany me round the sites for evening prayers.
The drifters would actually wait for her. She helped many a
man to darn his socks as I tried to help them to write letters.
In this respect I'd learned to advise a man to write as firmly as
he liked when in disagreement with home but *never* to post
the letter for two or three days. I knew by that time his wrath,
having been vented, would be likely to have spent itself, and
he would tear up the original letter and write another!

Sometimes those evening visits had their hazards due to
foul weather when I would do my 'rounds' on my own. It was
easy to stray off the worn path to huts and to walk into wet
peat where one's feet could sink easily and balance would be
lost. No lights could be seen and in winter weather it was dark
from about 3 PM Often, as I carried a little portable organ from
the roadway, I would stray from the path, stumble as one leg
became submerged in wet peat and, on withdrawing my foot
the gum-boot would remain behind. I then renewed my

imbalance by putting my foot back into the peat but with no boot! Once I knew I had walked too far and I flashed an emergency torch to find I was within a yard of the cliff edge – still carrying the organ!

Life on the island was not as we knew it on more ordinary stations. Isolation and lack of sporting and welfare amenities lead to very odd behaviour. Cricket was played on a rough strip of ground designated the pitch, stumps, bat and ball were all imaginary, but all the motions of village cricket were followed. One wretched fellow was pulled up for failing to salute an officer, but he explained that he had his dog on a lead and the dog was pulling too hard. There was neither dog nor lead! Target practice by the Navy was a familiar sight and we saw floating targets being towed along the Flow when but few ships were in. The targets had to survive and were not to be actually hit, but some of our anti-tank thought they would show the Senior Service how to shoot and, in one shot, blew a valuable target out of existence. On another occasion a shot bounced on the water, ricocheted and a splinter discomfited a woman who was bent low a she tethered a cow on South Ronaldsay Island. Poor soul, she had little comfort in her chair for some days after. A great friend of ours with whom I had worked in the Children's Special Service Mission at Bembridge was chaplain of one of the battleships (I will not identify it or him) and he suggested we walked the island (five by three miles) together, while he plotted a cross-country chase for the sailors. He then would provide them with a grand beer or tea meal in the naval canteen ashore. I enquired of the manager of the canteen how everything had gone and discovered that, course plotted, refreshments provided, the ship's company had never been informed of the chase and, of course, nobody had turned up.

I treasure the memory of a band concert late on a Sunday summer evening. It was on the Quarter Deck of the battleship *HMS King George V* and, as a very great honour to me, it had been timed after my Sunday services. The music on the water was wonderful and I can never sing 'The day Thou gavest, Lord, is ended' without remembering the closing number of that concert.

Everything done on the islands came into the category of secret. No cameras were allowed and this prevented a fascinating photograph being taken. As we understood it, some of the underwater defences had been blown up being, it was considered, no longer reliable. A few days later rumours spread of a very strange carcase being washed up on the island of Burray. Pat and I went first to smell and then to see a carcase which I can only describe as having the shape of a chicken about twelve feet in length, lying alongside but attached was a large sack-like feature looking like an enlarged stomach (six or seven feet long) and a twelve foot neck surmounted by a bovine shaped head. The locals were almost superstitious about it and suggested it was a killer whale! Because of secrecy conditions I could do nothing to discover if it was of very special interest. Its skin was covered in coarse brindled hair and its smell had prepared us for something unusual. Could it have been some form of pterodactyl?

One afternoon after about thirteen or fourteen months on the island I was surprised to find a signalman on the doorstep with orders for me to report for duty at Sandhurst! No surprise would have been greater or more unexpected. I knew it could not be 'promotion' to such a senior place, but it all sounded strangely different and, as it happened, led to promotion.

As we sailed past the Naval signalling station at Stanger Head a message was flashed across the water which – sadly – I was not to get for a few days. The message read 'Psalm 121, verse 8', 'The Lord shall preserve thy going out and thy coming in from this time forth and for evermore'.

Chapter VI
SANDHURST AND NORTH ALDERSHOT

My posting to Sandhurst and work there under D'Arcy Staunton (senior chaplain) was as rewarding as it was happy. My main care was with the HQ Company which maintained the tanks. Sandhurst was then the 100 RAC OCTU, training cadets as officers for cavalry regiments and Royal Tank Corps. I had additional chaplaincy duties in New College. But such divides were not absolute, nor were they intended to be, and one was fully part of Sandhurst's life. Pat and I found a small cottage in the village, Strawberry Cottage, and the path was well trodden or cycled between that and the RMA, by others as well as ourselves.

To move from the primitive provisions for worship as existed in the Orkneys to the magnificence of the Sandhurst Chapel was breathtaking. There were no acoustic aids and the full chapel demanded adjustments. I remember D'Arcy Staunton saying to me 'Place God reverently two thirds of the way back in the congregation and pray to Him there'. There in Sandhurst, chapel worship and military expertise met in a way I shall never forget.

I was detailed one Sunday to preach at the parade service at the Garrison Church of Marlborough Lines, near Aldershot. This church had originally been built as a 'Florence Nightingale' hospital alongside a riding school and the church was as bare and uncomfortable as might be imagined. The semicircular sanctuary had a door opening off each side of it and a sort of tramway ran under each door. It had been an early dual purpose church and the Roman Altar and the Anglican Holy Table gave place to one another as occasion demanded! I said to my ATS driver as we returned to Sandhurst 'Put that church in the Litany', 'What do you mean, Padre' she said and I replied 'From Marlborough Lines and all other such garrison churches, good Lord deliver us'. Within ten days I was its senior chaplain! In spite of my dismissive remarks about the church, the service had nevertheless been inspiring and the congregation was largely made up of Mons OCTU (161) the long established infantry of the RMA Sandhurst. My work included the RAC training establishment at Farnborough, the RAMC establishment at Mytchett and Keogh and the renowned 'glass house' – the military prison. It was in Aldershot that I first had responsibilities towards the WRAC.

I still remember my first talk/discussion with the girls who were, I think, as ill at ease as I was! I was still young and their humour was not lacking. I thought to ease the situation by sitting informally on the end of the trestle table at the head of the room – but the trestles had been moved close to one another in the centre and the table top and I landed on the floor. A good laugh eased the atmosphere but I found them less easy to 'draw out' than I found the men. An inspired thought was given to me and I told them to have their mending and knitting next time we met. They talked readily over their needles.

The work was perhaps slanted mostly on the Officer Cadet Training Unit (OCTU) and one met many cadets who were to progress to high responsibility. Their 'passing out' parade was their great occasion and with a certain amount of caution I invited them to an early morning service of dedication before the parade 'fell in'. Years afterwards I was thrilled to be asked to conduct the last of these services before the 161 returned to Sandhurst as the RMA once again.

To be at an OCTU widened one's view of army life. One saw the care taken by colonels of regiments in their acceptance of officers. Training was of the highest order from 'square bashing' under RSM Britten to top demands of military expertise. Character training was no small part of the OCTU's task. One met a number of great army leaders – Cunningham, Dempsey, Ritchie and others – who made it their job to visit the OCTU and meet the cadets who sought commissioning as officers to their regiments. The colonel of a regiment is not the CO of a battalion, but the highest responsible authority in that regiment, however many battalions it had. I had an amusing interlude at Mons with Regiment Sergeant Major Britten. During the offertory hymn at a Parade Service I had heard the 'quick march' order being given to the collectors at the back of the church. During the week I encountered the Regimental Sergeant Major and I asked him whether I had heard him give a command to the collectors at my Parade Service. He responded 'Sir,' and I said 'The Parade Service is my parade, not yours' to which he protested that the men must behave in an orderly manner, even in church. I replied 'You have less confidence in the discipline of drill which you instil in your men than I have'. 'But Sir . . . ' 'If I hear another command from you I will invite the men to open their necks and sit comfortably' 'Sir, you *couldn't* do that!' I heard no further commands. In the chapel at Sandhurst where senior staff were seated in the chancel, it was the Adjutant who gave the signal to the collectors to move forward simply by turning a page in his hymn book.

Meanwhile the war marched on and the struggles of North Africa held the greatest share of public interest. Of course counter-invasion of Europe had now become of prime importance but timing was of the essence and not a lot was given to the public to know of what was being planned for security reasons. Rumours multiplied, but those who knew had nothing to say. It was when rumours and guessing ceased that lesser mortals in army life knew that something significant was afoot.

On the family front, Pat and I had found a very pleasant house in Farnborough Park – Monksway, Pirbright Road – and this was rented until, to our very great delight, we knew that a baby was on the way. This meant, for Pat, extreme care for we had waited and prayed for such an event for six years. We gave up the house and moved into a delightful establishment run as a guest house, still in Farnborough Park. It was a place of peace and beauty in the setting of tree lined spreading lawns, but it was not the right place for a young and fit chaplain to make a proper contribution to the urgency of the day, neither was it for one to ask 'favours' in view of our expectation of the babe's arrival.

A posting order to report as senior chaplain of 43 (Inf) Wessex Division was scarcely a surprise and, despite its upheavals, both Pat and I thought it was a right and proper posting. It took me to Kent and took Pat to her parents who had given up their Surrey home and were living in a house in London in George Street which was in our possession.

With the arrival of the babe getting closer Pat's parents moved down to a sizeable holiday bungalow near Bognor Regis which had been built by my parents. Meanwhile, I reported to my new posting as senior chaplain 43 Wessex Infantry Division at Tenterden, Kent.

Chapter VII

NORMANDY

The 43rd Wessex Infantry Division HQ was stationed at Tenterden in Kent. This Division was highly trained under a distinguished divisional commander, General GI Thomas, and it was to him I reported. He was a man of rare ability whose rule was as feared as much as it was respected. My predecessor had been posted away with a broken leg and his predecessor had come to grief in disagreement with the General. Some few days after my taking up duties I received a call from the Assistant Chaplain General stationed at Reigate 'Have you seen your boss?' he asked enigmatically, when I said I had been kindly received he said 'I'm praying for you every day'. I wondered whether there might not have to be a fourth senior chaplain of the division in less than a month!

In fact GI Thomas (or Von Thoma as he was nicknamed) was an extremely fine commander but although hard on his operational staff he was very fair. I served under him to the end of the war and then, both he and I having been promoted, I served under him again during the early days of occupation of Germany. We once were at variance over looting when we had the Germans on the run. He said it would teach the Huns a lesson and I was running an opposition party to the practice, saying it would undermine discipline and integrity. I went to see him when the Germans capitulated and congratulated him and he said 'Padre, I have sent out the order – I have stopped the looting'. Years after and when he was still more senior he had the generosity to say to me that I had been right at that time of disagreement and that he had been wrong. He cared deeply for the well-being of his division in the matter of avoiding all unnecessary casualties, his attacks were brilliantly mounted through a thoroughly able staff but those in high office of command under him felt the tension of his care!

We were on the eve of departure for Normandy on day five when Pat presented me with a longed for baby daughter. Pat and her parents had gone down to Bognor Regis to be near Dr. Shipham, her consultant, for the baby's birth. I had gone to see the General about another matter and then asked if I might break the ten-mile restriction rule on movement in order to travel across to Bognor and see Pat and our baby Patricia. The ten-mile rule was a security provision in immediate advance of our move forward and also had to do with use of our vehicles which had been prepared for our landings in Normandy, hopefully in shallow water. I had my permission if I could use a non-waterproofed vehicle *but* I had to be back at 6 PM because 'Bertha', the code word for movement, would then be operative. Waterproofing of one's vehicle consisted of mastic being applied to all vulnerable parts of the engine and in an eight-foot vertically erected exhaust pipe being attached to the existing one to clear the top of the water when we drove off the landing craft on nearing shore.

By the time I returned I knew that Advance Tactical HQs was to move off at midnight and I was on the roadway wishing the men well. The General's car drew to a screeching halt and he called through the window 'Who's that?' I reported myself and he said 'How's your wife?' I shall never forget it.

During our time at Tenterden the Division had three Officers' Messes. 'A' Mess was that of the General and his senior operational command staff, 'B' and 'C' Messes housed the second flight of operational command. The ADC to the general was, however, included in 'A' Mess. The ADC was called into the General's office one morning and ordered 'Go down to Ashford Station this afternoon and meet your successor'. This was the first that Burton Parry knew about his replacement! The new ADC-to-be was duly met and 'refreshed' in Ashford before being driven up to an unofficial officers' club in Tenterden and further 'refreshed'. By dinner time he was in a state of more than partial liquidity when he was seated beside his new General. Having not a care in the world he ordered himself a bottle of claret – the last available bottle. When the General himself thought to order his usual bottle of claret there was not one available. Evelyn Waugh, for that was who the ADC designate was, proceeded to demonstrate how he would deploy an infantry division in action and, in doing so, deployed his bottle of claret in the General's lap. Next morning there was no contact between the General and his, possibly reluctant, ADC, but the interchange the following morning was interesting: 'Mr Waugh, I do not think you are the ADC I was seeking' was met with 'Mr Thomas, I do not think you are the General I was seeking'.

Perhaps I had occasion to see a side of General Thomas not ordinarily seen. As we got obviously near to 'D' Day, within a matter of weeks, he suggested that the chaplains might be advised about their preaching, mindful of the fact that in many cases they were preaching to men who were soon to die.

The chaplains constituted a splendid collection of godly men including two Baptists and one Methodist and together we had already endured a week's intensive training under canvas in January weather. Chaplains can endanger their men as well as themselves in any number of ways by being clueless in action.

I knew I had been too long out of the line. In Dunkirk days we had marched in fours, and now the army marched in threes, and field training had gone on apace while I was isolated in the Orkneys, and then differently orientated at Sandhurst and Marlborough Lines. The chaplains – with one exception – had had no battle experience, no practical skills in compass reading or map reading, no instruction as to car maintenance in matters of likely break-down etc. and I knew I needed to be clued up as much as they did. The staff officer who planned the course with me was Major Donald Wilson who afterwards was the person who produced *The Forsyte Saga* and *Anna Karenina*. We also had a session in church on the conduct of services and – knowing of his BBC expertise – I asked him to advise on voice production. He had a lot to say about 'the God voice' and his criticisms were valid.

We met later for a whole day conference, accepting the

invitation of the Vicar of Tenterden to use his church and study. Canon SM Warner from Eastbourne led us in devotional thought and prayer during the morning sessions and centred his talks on 1 Corinthians 13 'Though I speak . . . and have not love'. In the afternoon we faced together the solemn challenge of preaching sensitively to dying and endangered men. We spent a long time in silence, each prayerfully thinking what were the most urgent channels of approach and allowing ourselves a series of six sermons; we then collated these ideas and entrusted them to a very few who were to determine which sermon themes we would adopt. We all agreed to adhere to what emerged. Finally we knelt together in the vicar's study and solemnly offered our lives in the dangers ahead and covenanted that if we survived it was only to offer them again. Before we crossed the Seine we who had survived did the same thing again for the continuing task.

But to go back to D-Day once again and to our part in the Normandy landings. Tactical HQs having moved off from Tenterden at midnight, the remainder of the HQ followed in convoy at first light en route for the docks at Purfleet and on the way down drove through my father's old parish of St. John's which knit together the boundaries of Deptford, Lewisham and Brockley. The roads were lined with well-wishers and I half hoped that I might have recognised some. It was not to be. We dossed down in bare hutments at Purfleet and, in due course, settled down for the night. The first enemy plane overhead came nearer and nearer despite anti-aircraft fire then, quite suddenly, silence. Then came a heavy explosion and everyone cheered. A second, third and more planes followed in exactly the same pattern of behaviour and we

knew we were experiencing our first V1 rocket encounter –
the Buzz Bomb

We embarked on the *William S Jones*, which was one of the
special liberty ships very hastily assembled in the States and
used in large numbers for the occasion. It was a wonderful
achievement for, I believe, each was built each in about eight
weeks, but they were not built for comfort. We slept in the
holds and on deck and set off, passing safely through the
shelling we encountered through the Straits of Dover overnight. The officers had an area apportioned to them to lay out
their valises in No.1 Hold and I asked myself whether it
would be ostentatious to kneel and pray as normally I did
before turning in. Finally I propped myself quite openly
against the bulkhead, sitting upright with New Testament in
hand, read a few verses, prayed, and then turned in. The next
night another officer asked if he might join me and by the time
we disembarked at the Normandy landings my New
Testament had been in use by five or six officers, all sitting
upright against the bulkhead.

Food was a monotonous repetition of Compo Pack K,
which in itself was excellent – spam and plum pudding – but
doled out for every meal for some five days became ever less
enjoyable on an unsteady boat. We were also issued with a
nightly tin of first-rate self-heating soup. It looked like any
other soup tin except that it had a small pad on top which
gave enough heat and more to warm the contents of the tin
when touched by a match or lighted cigarette.

The ship's crew was obviously under stress and kept themselves strictly to themselves. We were unceremoniously forbidden the use of their lavatory facilities. The deck was our

province and we could adjust accordingly. Our mouths and gums were raw from the hard-tack biscuits which were the traditional ratings' bread in previous days in the Navy, and the smell of baking fresh bread being baked for the crew tantalised us from time to time. On deck one day I was standing by a raw and junior officer of the watch and I remarked on the impressive view we had of the *Rodney* battleship nearby. With disdain and dislike in his voice he replied 'If the *Nelson* has on its bows the word "Rodney", then it is a good view of the *Rodney*'. I said firmly 'Train your glass on it'. His face looked a picture of dismay: 'Next time' I said 'look at the ACK-ACK mountings before you try to be clever!' He was not to know that I knew nothing about anti-aircraft mountings beyond the fact that they were different, but I did know the camouflage designs from my days in Scapa Flow.

Two things I shall long remember from those days. First the depth of sincerity of the crowded No. 3 Hold deck when we all had morning prayers and a short devotional talk and secondly our relief when at last the troubled waters would allow us to disembark. 'Troops Landing Crafts' came alongside in succession and our vehicles were loaded on to their decks which had space for vehicles facing forward two by two. The bow of each craft was a flat landing ramp and this was lowered to water level as near shore as was thought safe. Vehicle by vehicle we hit the water on full engine revs hoping that the speed we had achieved and the spin of the wheels would carry us far enough to touch bottom before we floundered. 'Poor devils' the British Naval Officer said to me as I climbed onto my Jeep whose floor was three sandbags deep against mine splinter penetration and I replied 'You don't know how glad I shall be to have firm ground under my feet'. The water around us was bespeckled by floating dead bodies and army equipment and one's heart bled for those 'who had not made it'.

Twenty or so years later I saw the *William S Jones* alongside the harbour wall at Tripoli – well done its builders.

We landed without enemy opposition, enemy coastal guns had been silenced and enemy infantry and tanks were being engaged about a mile behind the shoreline.

In Normandy the AQ asked me if there were any chaplains I wished to recommend for decoration or award whose work had been outstanding. I replied that all had given of their best. Had any carried in wounded under fire? I asked how many times a day did he mean? He told me later that every chaplain had been recommended for decoration by his commanding officer and their brigadiers. Awards were given to Brigades for allocation and they were normally divided between regiments, so the chaplains did not 'fit' into the scheme. Nobody looked for awards, and brigadiers, all of whom spoke to me of their chaplains, did not feel entitled themselves to reduce an allocation to regiments in favour of chaplains. Should I have asked the AQ in the first case for an allocation, however small, for chaplains? I hope I did not let them down, none of them even hinted that I might have done so.

There was, however, one chaplain – Eric Gethyn-Jones whose gallantry was at sea just before his ship sank drowning two squadrons of our Recce Regiment, the Gloucesters. He had gone down into the flooded 'holds' of the ship helping men out and using a form of stretcher having a specialised operation he had only learned the previous day. I took advice

as to what award I should seek for Eric and was told that a
Military Cross would not be appropriate since we had not yet
actually joined battle. I put his name forward for a George
Medal and heard no more. After enquiry I was informed that
the 'powers that be' had forwarded the recommendation as
worthy of a George Cross and that it has been further recommended for a Victoria Cross, only to be turned down at that
level. Anyone whose name is put forward but is not awarded
a VC gets nothing. I discussed this with General Thomas and
he agreed that a new submission should be made on the
grounds that the chaplain's name had not initially been forwarded for more than a George Medal. The 'powers that be'
decided that perhaps he should receive an Order and since his
rank was that of Captain he received no more than an MBE.

By the end of hostilities it was decided that Commander in
Chief's Certificates should be given to outstanding personnel
who had not been recognised by decoration or award, and
this and Mentions in Despatches became the only other
'recognitions' which the chaplains received.

One regiment, just before the war ended, devised a regimental 'Cad's Army' in which anyone who did anything particularly foolish was awarded a Cad's Army Certificate or
decoration. By this time we were no longer digging trenches
to sleep in but had moved into empty houses where possible,
despite their being in ruins and without sanitation. One chaplain – a fine scholar who later held a senior professorship –
moved his kit into a ruined village house and found himself
accommodation on the first floor. In the morning he emptied
slops out of his window over an unfortunate soldier who was
in the wrong place at the wrong time. For that he was

awarded a Commander in Chief's Certificate in the Cad's
Army, but within an hour he held another and real
Commander in Chief's Certificate for his outstanding service.

Those early days in Normandy were, for many, their
baptism of fire and it proved again and again the value of the
training they had undergone. We, as chaplains, had had some
very hard training not long after the divisional course I had
arranged at Tenterden. We knew what the crack or the whine
of bullets meant, we knew that we could go on when natural
weariness would obviously have slowed us down. Night and
day frequently spelt action and we found that to throw
oneself down for a half-hours rest whatever the time was very
effective. Every time we moved as a unit or HQ our first task
was to dig a slit trench and there we slept when conditions
allowed. Soon conditions did allow, just as soon as we had
secured our bridgehead, but the necessity of slit trenches per-
tained all through the campaign.

There was humour too, even in danger. We were dug in at
first near Bayeux, almost within sight of Carpiquet airport
which remained in enemy hands, and frequently we had to
drive our vehicles within full view of their guns. Royal
Military Police signs were on the roadway

IF YOU ARE GOING EAST
MOVE FAST OR YOU WILL GO WEST

I was privileged to have a radio in my Jeep and I used to get
back to Div. HQs whenever I could in time for men to gather
round, have evening prayers and hear the news. Our prayers
(and short talk/sermonette) were interrupted one evening as

we saw an attack going in on Carpiquet airport nearby. A plane flew low over us to 'set the trail' and this was followed by bombers which we counted in and out. It was then time for the news and we heard an exact description of the raid we had just seen.

Chapter VIII

NORMANDY TO VICTORY

The Division's progress was later marked by the mayors of Maltot and Eterville who erected a monument on Hill 112 bearing the words 'To the 5th Devon and Cornwall Light Infantry and the 43rd Wessex Division who here decided the fate of the world'. When hostilities were over I flew down with the Divisional Commander for him to unveil and for me to dedicate a stone memorial less extravagantly worded.

Official records tell of the Division's exploits in the Bocage country, over Mount Pincon, securing our sector of the Falaise Gap, on to crossing the Seine, hurried progress through Holland and through the flooding caused by the enemy breaching of dykes, on to the relief of the Parachutists across the Rhine at Arnhem, through attack after attack down to Rees where we crossed the Rhine. This series of attacks was outstanding, making history. GI Thomas was advised as we fought our way to Rees that the Brigades were totally exhausted and that the men might 'crack' under the strain, but GI knew his men and their gallant morale and replied

'Crack, of course the men will crack, but it will be the Bosch', and so it was.

These memoirs are not intended to tell the story of the Division's history, others have done this with professional skill. My memories of those days are without diary and are only personal touches of things that happened en route.

In battle when a special attack is planned there is an Order of Battle which enumerates which troops have been designated to take part. Thus the 43rd Division was under command of 12 Corps, then 1st Corps, then the Canadian Army and then again 1st Corps. Our own General was responsible for the deployment of the Brigades and to make demand from the Army for armoured support and for specialised troops such as Bridging Companies and other Royal Engineer skills outside the 'norm' of our Divisonal Engineers. We were placed under command of the 2nd Canadian Army to break through the famous Siegfried Line.

While still in Normandy we had a Baptist casualty (George Mann) through appendicitis and this chaplain's replacement (also a Baptist) was of a somewhat sensitive, even timid, nature. He was finding his way round the company's lines using the hedges for cover as he had been taught when he fell into a land drain of extreme odour. The poor fellow pulled himself out, felt he could see nobody in his condition and so stripped off his clothes and laid them out in the sun to dry and lose a little of their odour. Had the enemy spotted this? Within minutes a mortar bomb exploded on the ditch and although the chaplain survived he had nothing to wear.

Three chaplains lost/gave their lives. The storming of Mount Pincon was led by the 5th Wilts whose commanding officer was Lt. Col. 'Pop' Pearson He wore a rose for his regiment the Lancashire Fusiliers and was armed only with a walking stick. He knew he was leading a suicidal attack which would cost the regiment (5th Wiltshires) very dear, scores of dead and hundreds of wounded. The CO himself, his second in command, the adjutant, doctor and chaplain were among the dead. Jimmy Douglas, the chaplain, was loved by all ranks and deeply mourned. I had been with him and we had prayed together as the attack was forming up, he was killed within the next quarter of an hour. Much later on another dear chaplain, a Welshman Tal Davis, had his lower spine shot away and took a tragically long time to die. I sat with him inwardly weeping but thanking God that the physical shock had diminished the pain. The third chaplain to die, Fred Musgrave, was replacing a battle casualty. I had driven him up to join the regiment as it was reaching a new location and it had been spotted in movement by the enemy. A shell landed on Battalion HQ as I left but I had not anticipated casualties. On my way back I, too, was spotted and a self-propelled gun had a few 'gos' at me, finally blowing me into the ditch.

I think my most dramatic moment was on Nijmegan Bridge. I had been visiting on foot near Elst and had parked my jeep near a farmhouse knowing there was no adequate 'cover'. They had a few 'gos' at me as I drove to the bridge which I chanced to reach as a dive bomber was flying overhead. The roadway danced with tongues of fire, an incredible sight, and 'you couldn't see me for smoke'. This sort of thing happened in all the chaplains' experiences – one found himself driving in his jeep between two German panzer tanks who never recognised him for what he was, another lost the contents of his trouser pocket but only had a burning scratch, I was lightly buried by a mortar bomb in a slit trench with a few Dorset Regiment soldiers and we helped each other out.

There was, however, an occasion when visiting a battalion which had just come out of the line and whose men were resting in slit trenches questionably out of range. A sergeant asked me if I really believed in prayer and whether a chap should pray. It was a familiar question but he had something to share with me. He had been under fire, heavy fire, the night before but he wasn't going to pray. He didn't believe in it; if the shell had got his name on it so be it, if not, well, 'what the hell'! One shell, however, had arrived, it did not have his name on it, but it had his address. He then began to pray and he was delighting in the conviction that God was real.

There was another occasion which, like the last, I frequently tell at Remembrance Day services. I think it was in the Worcester Regiment lines where I met a young soldier in tears outside the Regimental Aid Post. It was his pal, he said, they had grown up together, joined the army together and both were stretcher bearers. They had gone out for a wounded man and the enemy had 'got' his pal 'They got my pal, Padre – they got my pal'. I said 'Did you get the wounded lad in son?' 'Yes, Padre, or I'd have let my pal down'.

These contacts with our troops were not haphazard. Each morning I would pray that I might be given something – a thought for the day – not only for myself, but a 'thought' to share. We were all facing danger and this daily thought in its freshness bound us together as we had a short prayer.

Among all the unsung heroes of battle I would place the

Royal Military Police (the red caps) very high on my list. Too often they are associated with discipline of dress and behaviour, but in battle where vehicles are apt to bunch approaching dangerous places such as busy cross-roads and village squares, or perhaps are tempted to rush such places and cause traffic congestion, there we always found an RMP controlling the traffic himself, standing in the very centre of the target of shell fire and sharing his steadiness of nerve with all who passed his post.

How many stories there are to tell of sadness and humour and of risks which were taken by all almost without thought. The Normandy roadways were thickly mined and our gallant engineers had cleared a path in the centre of the roads. We all took it in turn to move off the centre as we encountered vehicles going the other way. I shall always remember a story told by Lord Mancroft of when he was a Battery Commander in a famous regiment which was clearing the beaches of Normandy. Lord Dowding had come across to see and share the danger of the landings, covered as they so well were by the RAF, and as an Air Marshal he took his stand among others on the foreshore. A battery sergeant major was leaning on his shovel open mouthed looking at the Air Marshal. 'Battery Sergeant Major' said his Battery Commander, 'have you never seen an Air Marshal before? Why don't you salute?' 'Yes sir, but I've never seen a real live Air Marshal before standing on a real live Teller mine!'

When one looks back on days of combat one naturally enjoys memories of the fellowship which was so real between comrades under great strain; and memories of gallantry, too, illuminate those grim years of horror and carnage. The stench

of the battlefield when the weather was hot, the bodies
bloated in death and so unlike what the body looked like in
health. Burial was an urgent problem, but should one go into
a mined area to retrieve a body already dead? My instructions
to the chaplains were never to risk their lives for a dead body.
The chaplain serving with his regiment moved as the regiment moved and *never* deserted regimental lines. He buried,
helped invariably by others, near where the body lay but in
an identifiable place, such as the corner of a field, and he
marked the grave with a labelled improvised cross, sending
an eight-figure map reference to the Graves Registration Unit
and enclosing a letter to the next of kin. These letters were
held back until official notice of death had been sent to the
next of kin but were very often movingly and gratefully
acknowledged.

In the 43rd Division we devised a scheme which worked
reasonably well. The Provost Marshal (chief policeman) and I
would agree a place for the prisoners of war 'cage' before any
particular battle joined. I was apportioned a small team under
an NCO; we would mark out a cemetery near the POW cage
and as prisoners came in they were directed to dig the graves.
Poor wretches, they often feared they were digging their own.
Ration trucks (which were metal lined) took the rations up
daily to the nearest possible spot where their contents would
be available for distribution, and they would return via our
cemetery with such bodies as were not buried 'on the field'.
The chaplains of any battalions in reserve took burial duties
each night. There was an occasion when I found two cavalry
officers (for chaplain or officers might well come down with
their dead) in anxious discussion with one of the chaplains on

duty. The dead man had had himself designated 'atheist' on his identity disk. Could he be given Christian burial? I asked the officers whether they thought this was a determined atheist or perhaps a lad expressing youthful independence. They replied 'Padre, there are no atheists now left in the regiment!'

Very occasionally the advance of battle left too many casualties behind for chaplains to cope with. The mined fields in the Bocage country were fought through at high speed and both our own dead and enemy dead were left behind sprawled over walls and hut windows and often still with rifle almost in hand. Our engineers had marked probably all the mines and, in a sense as SCF, such dead became my responsibility. I was given a posse of twenty German prisoners under a German sergeant and all under the supervision of two armed soldiers to do what could be done. The prisoners were newly 'in' and were unfit to do much, being sick as they touched the dead. I found I was heavily involved and we dragged as many bodies as we could to a trench where we laid them side by side. Through their NCO, who spoke English, I asked that any Christians among the prisoners would raise their hands. None did. I then said I did not mind what religion they had on their identity disks, but would they pray with me so that, together in German and English, we would pray the Lord's Prayer, then I would pray for peace, for all bereaved, and for all being hurt in the conflict. A few hands went up – to be followed by all. We marched back to the POW cage and the NCO fell his men in in front of me and gave me the only Nazi salute I ever got. I hope I did not show it but, for the moment, I feared that Nazi salute was a mark of defiance.

An earlier burial of a soldier on the German border was attended by some of his comrades. One of these was the twin brother of the dead soldier and he asked if he might be part of the burial service and offer an extempore prayer. It was a deeply moving experience.

On a happier note, I recall that just after we had crossed the Seine the nation was called to a Service of Thanksgiving. General Thomas said to me 'Padre, be careful what you say in this service, the war is not over', I said 'Sir, I am not preaching at this service, you are! You know better than any to what degree the Division has cause to give thanks'. His face was worth a pound a minute! 'I'll tell you on Thursday' was what he said and I said we would have the sermon immediately following the reading of the Lesson. We were all very moved in Divisional HQs the following Sunday.

When we had crossed the Seine, the Guards Armoured Division was given our heavy transport to carry fuel for them in their rush forward into Brussels. We were grounded temporarily at Vernon. Everyone had, of necessity, been travelling light and chaplains had told me that they were finding it hard to get Communion Wine. The 'vin ordinaire rouge' gave one a shock in a Communion Cup and there was nothing better to purchase. I still had my jeep and I decided to go to Paris accompanied by a fellow chaplain and a newly joined lieutenant colonel staff officer. I had to get a 'bon' from the Church for the purchase of wine and denominational differences just did not exist in the warmth of how I was received. Finally I had to go to a very senior priest (equivalent Archdeacon) of the Paris diocese. He gave me a 'bon' of such dimension that I could have floated a ship in it and a dear elderly lady on his staff (as she bade me farewell) insisted that I accepted from her a small block of her unbelievably precious chocolate. I was deeply moved and embarrassed, but despite protest I had to accept it.

Paris was actually out of bounds to the British but in bounds to the Americans and, as we walked down the Champs Elysée, whom should we see having a drink outside one of the cafés but the General, the commanding Gunner Brigadier and I forget who else. My companions said 'Take cover, quick' but rightly or wrongly I said 'No' and I went up and made my salute. The next day I was sent for and asked what was I doing in Paris, did I not know it was out of bounds? – he then proceeded to tell me why he was there! A day or two later I was with the Gunner brigadier in his car and I said 'I don't think the General liked seeing me in Paris' 'Not that' he said 'he didn't like your seeing him'. Nevertheless, I was given permission to return to Paris to collect the Communion Wine as arranged on our earlier visit.

Hope of home leave was at this time an enormous cheer to all of us in action. The journeying was tedious but so well worth while and England seemed fair indeed. My parents were still in the Rectory at Tooting and they had converted the cellars of the house into a public air raid shelter retaining a very small corner for the family. The whole area was bunk-bedded but I seem to remember their arranging of teas or coffee to be available and I remember the snoring! A 'good-night prayer' was offered at approximately ten o'clock. This latter I was asked to offer when I was at home.

Pat's parents had given up their home in Outwood, Surrey, having lost their gardener and household younger staff to the war effort. They were occupying the lower half of a house I had in George Street just looking on to Bryanston Square. Pat was looking after them and helping her mother to do the cooking! Her mother had never cooked but Pat had done a short course on house maintenance before she married an impecunious parson! It so happened that I was with them on the night that the Germans made a vicious firebombing attack on the West End. We took refuge, as was the custom, on the stairs leading down to the basement with stirrup pumps at the ready lest our house would get a direct hit. The swish of landing bombs was a new experience to me and made me realise that those we sought to protect were in every way living as much endangered lives as we were – and they on short rations.

Restaurants at home were not expensive but they made more realistic profits on drinks, coffees and 'extras'. I remember the Criterion, The Hungarian, the Café Royal and other fine restaurants supplying dinner at three shillings and sixpence (the maximum allowed) the equivalent of just under twenty pence in today's money. Other restaurants – Lyons' 'Piccadilly Pop', now the premises of Simpsons, charged two shillings and sixpence, (i.e. twelve-and-a-half pence) for a six or seven course dinner and Lyons Cafés and Corner Houses even less.

At last came the surrender on Luneberg Heath. The German Field Marshal refused to hand over his baton to a less senior officer who finally snatched it from him and broke it in two on the German's head. Of course he got a reprimand for this, but General Horrocks and finally George VI both held part of this trophy.

Casualties after the war continued as booby traps and

mined bridges and other such hazards still persisted, and
these casualties had a poignant tragedy all of their own.

We had begun to see 'surrenders' from the time we crossed
the Rhine and it was then I had a strange experience for a
chaplain. We were told that two airmen had been shot down
near a village just a short distance from us and short of the
Rhine and I decided that, with the help of our Dutch inter-
preter, that if possible we would find their graves and ensure
that they were marked. As we came into the village in just the
one jeep, sheets were hung out of windows, people waved
white towels and the village head man – whatever he was –
came to me carrying a huge key. I didn't know what to do! I
accepted the key, shook him by the hand, and handed the key
back. We all parted good friends.

In company with the same Dutch officer I had previously
nearly got into serious and stupid trouble. Ours had been a
stop-and-go progress towards the Rhine as we awaited the
skill of our sappers to replace blown up bridges. We had
passed across the Dortmund Emms canal an hour or so back
and we knew we had a six-hour wait. The Dortmund Emms
canal was decorated with some splendid boathouses and I
commented to the Dutch Liaison Officer how tempting they
looked. 'Was I game for a row' was how my remark was
taken. We found an open boathouse with an uncoxed pair in
it and without a care in the world we set off. I suppose we had
been rowing half an hour or so when the Dutchman said 'Do
you feel comfortable . . . I think we are in enemy lines!' We
turned about and I had not even strength to feather my blade
by the time we reached the boat house. His input was greater
by far than mine. I knew I had only rowed in the Jesus College

rugger boat when up at Cambridge, I did not know that he had rowed for his country!

We finished our part of the war in Celle where we had a wonderful thanksgiving service in the old Stadt Kirche which was packed to the doors with every Divisional unit represented. We had a splendid young office of the DCLI (Duke of Cornwall's Light Infantry) whom I knew slightly as a liaison officer between 214 Brigade and Divisional HQs and whom I had discovered was no ordinary musician. The organist of the Stadt Kirche was not prepared to make his magnificent organ, on which Brahms had played, available to a soldier. But we had won the war and the soldier was wearing shoes, not army boots, when I took him to view the instrument. With the utmost reluctance the organist unlocked the console shutters and then watched with growing interest as the stop combinations were selected and penetrating questions were asked in German. What he did not know was that the soldier he had tried to spurn had been the Organ Scholar at King's College, Cambridge, David Wilcocks. On my eightieth birthday David sent me the copy of that service on which he had made his notes – a really generous thought.

I first got to know David Wilcocks when conducting a Christmas Service for the DCLI Christmas Service in the cellars of a cement factory and I asked if they had anyone who could play my little collapsible organ. They produced David Wilcocks and I said 'I hear you play' and he simply replied 'Yes'. Most people would have said 'I'll have a bash' or something similar. 'How does it work' David asked, he'd never seen anything like it. I explained that it was like riding a bicycle as far as the pedals were concerned. He touched a note and said 'Not a bad tone', but when he began to play I couldn't believe my ears. It was only after that service that I discovered who he was – for little did I know that he was to become the world-renowned musician, Sir David Wilcocks.

Chapter IX
POST-WAR IN GERMANY

Those were terrible days for the German people and there was a spirit of forlorn despair in many devastated places. General Thomas ordered that no help was to be given to any citizen of Cologne who had not cleared the rubble and mess from the immediate front of his or her doorway – this he told me was to encourage them to achieve some self-respect. The general public naturally looked on us with envy and if our behaviour lacked discipline then we lost their respect. There was a sad breakdown on our part in regard to alcohol. Rhine wines were available at sixpence (two-and-a-half pence) per bottle and champagne at half a crown (twelve-and-a-half pence) and there was every occasion for celebration, especially as officers were recalled home for demobilisation. Many such officers were routed through the Ruhr and were temporarily attached to units en-route. Each stop spelt another occasion for release celebration and the shameful result was seen in the defeated German soldiery having to carry drunken British officers onto the boats bound for the United Kingdom.

I made a bold report on this to Rhine Army and was summoned to appear before my Corps Commander who was the same General Thomas of 43 Division., now promoted to be Lieut. General commanding 1st Corps. (Major General is short for Sergeant-Major General and this is therefore a junior rank to Lieut.General.) His desk was clear and we talked informally about the Corps, its morale and certain less happy areas. Then from under his blotting pad he disclosed the copy of my report to Army HQs which I had sent him. 'You stand by this?' he said. He went on 'I can see you are familiar with the Corps but remember I am even more so – and you stand by your report?' With real sadness I looked him in the eye and said 'I do'. There was a pause and then he said 'I'm sorry . . . but I agree with you'. He took effective measures which curtailed the abuse, forbidding farewell parties of more than twelve people unless specific permission had been granted by him.

Another problem arose out of black market practices. All army personnel had a free issue of cigarettes. Cigarettes and chocolate etc. were available to us from NAAFI. Cigarettes could buy anything from sex to cameras and apart from a host of responsible people, there were some who found themselves under unfair pressures. Being a non-smoker I found I had accumulated an enormous quantity of cigarettes and I used these as 'packing' when the time came for us to receive a posting home. HM Customs were intrigued and asked me to estimate the number, they charged me not-too-much on what I really didn't want.

Again, there was the question of currency and the effect of British currency circulating in Germany. We were issued instead with BAFS currency and the rate of exchange was totally unfair to us. We were not to overspend in Germany, but this represented no benefit to us.

German needs were sometimes shamefully exploited as happened on a roadway near Hamm. Two soldiers stopped one of the very rare German cars and offered the driver a jerrycan full of petrol (five gallons) for a costly sum. Further along the road the car was stopped again and searched. After bribes were accepted the car moved on and the confiscated petrol was returned to starting point! Need I say the device was soon discovered and due punishment meted out! Worse things happened on the east of our sector when a YMCA canteen was stolen by Russian soldiers. Representations were made at a high level and we were told that the thieves had been identified and executed but that the canteen could not be found. I suspected the truth of both statements.

Brighter and happier memories remain. In Iserlohn the German Lutheran Church made available to us one of their most lovely churches. Later they sought to reinstall a truly valuable reredos which was of heavy Germanic emphasis. I hope I was right, but I declined that reredos in favour of the more simple arrangements which we had already in use. Again in Iserlohn, Pat was stopped by a German woman who asked if it was she who had given some chocolate to her children (a forbidden thing). 'I can never thank you enough' the woman said.

A NAAFI story which I got second-hand from Bad Einhausen, where German girls were employed behind the counters, told of a British wife who had asked for a rabbit. The girl flung a large Belgian hare on the counter. 'That's not a rabbit, that's a hare!' was the shocked reaction. The German girl turned it over disdainfully saying 'I don't know, it might be herr or it might be fraulein'!

Despite all the side issues which could either hurt or amuse, our role was a serious one. We were to be responsible people in a country which we had cruelly, but of necessity, brought to its knees. Nazi-ism had evidenced the spirit of anti-Christ, there were places where crosses were twisted into swastikas and where the loveliness of youth had been twisted into horror. Fraternisation was strictly forbidden lest it occur at a low level, but fraternisation at high level could have proved of enormous value.

People have asked why the Allies did not go straight on to Berlin as they so easily could have done and as we anticipated doing earlier in the campaign. The reason was, as I was told at a high level, the Allies had agreed that Russia should be allowed this distinction as we wanted their goodwill and co-operation if we had to invade Japan. For this, the availability of Vladivostok would have been of enormous significance.

My promotion to Deputy Assistant Chaplain General (DACG) 1st British Corps covering the Ruhr was as unexpected as it was undeserved, and I felt dwarfed by the task of accepting responsibility for so many chaplains under whose guidance I would have been more than happy to serve. There were some 220 chaplains in the Corps area, which was vast, and they were all men who had proved their worth, and proved their courage too. My posting at 1st Corps saw the arrival of my wife Pat with our two year old daughter 'Tricia who came out on one of the first troop ships to transport wives after the war. The presence of wives introduced a new and more gentle spirit into what had been a theatre of war.

The Ruhr was 'flat' and to fly over it was to see how great the devastation was with not a roof's cover in sight. What houses remained were empty shells whose cellars provided the only accommodation. Wood blocking on the roads had been burnt away by aerial bombing and we frequently drove our staff cars on the surviving tram-lines which stood 'proud' in the street rubble. The great bridges at Cologne were up-ended ramps into the Rhine and it was impossible to discover among the Germans who were truly our enemies and who had grown to distrust Nazi rule.

We had a chaplains' conference centre just outside Iserlohn in a woodland hotel where we allowed very limited accommodation to the displaced proprietor and his family. Here we had opportunity to run courses for serving personnel as well as for chaplains. Iserlohn Church House provided a seed-bed for Christian faith and a nursery garden for people in whom the stresses and strains of war had awakened their sense of and need of their God. One of our outstanding wardens was afterwards to become Professor ARC Leaney – who had been an outstanding chaplain of 43rd Division.

We fitted into our Church House programme an interesting gathering of German clergy for a few days' conference where we discussed the urgency of Evangelism in a broken society. In fact we had a further, and hidden, purpose in inviting these clergy to meet some of us chaplains. I approached General Thomas and asked if I might have present a selected few senior officers on the 'supply' side of the Corps. German clergy found it well nigh impossible to meet the needs of their work, and travel was impossible because they had no entitlement to petrol. Communications were likewise frustrated because there was no availability of paper. It was urgent that we helped. Sensitive senior staff experts would learn a lot as they sat amongst us unofficially. General Thomas willingly acquiesced but asked 'how are these German clergy to be fed?' He knew that the British press was ever vigilant and would highlight any irregularities. They would bring their ration cards with them, I replied, and after the conference they would have them returned to them – unused! But this was not for the General to know officially for he might well have been under attack for it.

Many Germans had claimed to be clergy in order to gain early release to home going from POW cages and these had been screened by our security authorities and their number had reduced to some 100–150 if I rightly remember. David Strangeways (finally and many years after to be ordained) was the Senior Security Officer in 1st Corps. He asked me to screen the final numbers of the German POW clergy and I agreed, provided that I might select a fellow chaplain who spoke German and that I be allowed to have a trusted – ie non political – German pastor in attendance to advise. I was put in touch with a godly and delightful Pastor Busch of Düsseldorf. The fellow chaplain I selected was ARC (Bob) Leaney and our experience in this task was sobering.

- The SS carried no chaplains
- The Wehrmacht had one 'regular' chaplain per division of 13,000 men
- German soldiers had to wear uniform at all times but a uniformed German soldier was not allowed into a civilian church.

- Clergy were conscripted as ordinary soldiers into the German army and were not entitled to conduct worship

Some of the clergy we interviewed were broken and saddened people who had kept no contact with their civilian congregations and had actually hidden the fact that they were clergy. I submitted a report to higher authority.

Those early days in post-war Germany still held a degree of danger as well as enjoyment. For the most part the Germans were subservient and anxious for employment and security, but still there was cruelty about. Travel for Germans returning to their homes was extremely difficult. Thumbing a lift was well nigh impossible and civilian trains were rare in the extreme. I remember seeing a man literally thrown out of a carriage at Hamm when he tried to enter it – and room could have been made for him. Travel for us could, in places, be hazardous. This I discovered when I tried to hurry back to base on a forbidden autobahn as light was failing. There was no bridge where I expected to find one! I skidded to a standstill sideways on to an ugly drop. The reason for my taking the risk that I did was that occasionally people found wire stretched across a darkened road at head height. Our jeeps were uncovered except for a loose canvas sheet which, in foul weather, we could attach to the top of the windscreen but, more often than not, we tilted the windscreen level to the bonnet. This had been normal practice during fighting days in order to preclude their flashing reflection in the sun which would have attracted enemy attention. All our vehicles now had angle-iron brackets fitted in front of their radiators and standing to a height above that of the driver to deal with such wire as might otherwise cause decapitation.

We saw something of the indescribable horror of concentration camps, for Belsen was only 12 miles away from 43 Division HQs, and I also saw a lethal and cruel air missile which was never finally used by the enemy. This was at Dannenburg where under camouflage we found a factory that was making V4s. These aircraft were V1s, but each with a pilot, so that its landing would be on target when its engines cut out. We were told that POWs would be the pilots, whose death would be a certainty, but we wondered whether they might not be piloted by willing, or even unwilling, German personnel.

Everything, however, was to change as the months went by and the number of British troops in Germany was to diminish through army release.

'How are the mighty fallen and the weapons of war perished.' I was to revert from what we sometimes called 'press-fastener' rank to where I now belonged properly on the Army List. In other words, I was no longer to be CF 2nd Class (Lieut.Col. equivalent) but to be CF 3rd Class (Major). I was posted home as Senior Chaplain, Guards Depot, Caterham in 1947.

Chapter X

CATERHAM

The preliminary training of both regular and national service Guardsmen began at Caterham and then continued at Pirbright, not far from Aldershot. Trainees came into Caterham's depot as boys and approximately sixteen weeks later passed out as men. Squad by squad under excellent non-commissioned officers, they went through intensive training which, some would say, broke them before it made them. Drill instruction, physical training, personal discipline were all part of their training and the place of Christian faith was an important ingredient. The chaplains, seldom in military uniform, were free to mingle at every level and we were privy to the struggle which the lads went through 'Do you remember me, Padre?' was said quietly to me years later when I was a guest in a Guards Officers' Mess in the Canal Zone and was being passed a dish of 'eats'. 'I was the recruit who wept on your shoulder at the Depot.' He was but one of many who knew what it was to come to the end of courage and endurance and then to find he could go on and win through. Many times I rang through to Company Office to the Company Sergeant Major asking how recruit 'X' was doing? 'He's OK, Padre. You want me to know something?' 'Well, he's a bit disheartened and uncertain of himself.' 'Thank you, Padre, I'll find occasion to give him some commendation.' Just occasionally the recruit would be thoroughly unsatisfactory and the answer had to be found in a different way. Quite often it was that a Company Commander (each of the Foot Guards had a Company in training at the Depot) would ring saying 'Recruit "X" was marched before me this morning, I had to put him in detention'. 'Would you go and see him, I think he has a problem'. The Sergeant of the Guard Room, Sergeant George, would put the fear of death into anybody because of a damaged throat and hard voice, but he had a heart of gold. One lad he had in detention, who had cut his wrist in total depression, was 'Not a bad lad, Padre. I've got him looking after my chickens and he will be OK in no time'.

Squad by squad they came to receive Christian instruction at the back of the chapel and very simply we shared with them the reality of God and God's care for them. They volunteered for Confirmation instruction in large numbers, and this they accepted as 'under orders' in the first place for once they had volunteered I would actually summon them. Everything in the Depot was ordered, but not as inflexibly as might be thought. When recruits volunteered for Confirmation instruction it was understood between us that they would appear three times without default and then if they wanted to 'drop out' I would accept that I was not 'getting through' and perhaps they would give another chaplain the chance to reach to them later in their career. After confirmation classes we chaplains saw candidates on their own before presenting them for confirmation. I asked one candidate, tall and well-built even among guardsmen 'What do you really want your confirmation to mean for you?' He replied 'I'm giving my lit-tleness to God's greatness'. Some squads agreed to go further in Christian practice. The whole squad would remain quiet in their barrack room at night after the Officer-in-Waiting had inspected them. They sat on the ends of their beds, whether to pray or just to be still. The prayer was 'O Lord, teach me some-thing from my Bible.' They had an issue of a New Testament or perhaps a more informal Gospel as given by the Scripture Gift Mission and received through the chaplain. Then the second prayer 'O Lord, whom shall I pray for at home or here in the Depot?' Lastly, the third prayer 'O Lord, is there any-thing I can do for you here in the Depot?' All this lasted just three minutes and there was a timekeeper appointed to say 'Time, gentlemen, please'. How many squads actually did this I do not know, but some did, and Officers-in-Waiting (Duty Officers) told me of the strange silence which followed their leaving the barrack room rather than the usual hubbub of noise.

Once we had a ghost in the Depot which caused a stir. A guardsman 'trained soldier' had been attending seances of some sort in either Croydon or Purley and he was, so it was thought, responsible for some strange occurrences. These latter we sorted out and the Commandant let it be known that any other ghosts would go straight into the Guard Room.

There was also an occasion when one recruit had the courage to complain at an unfortunate occurrence in the dining hall – 'Any complaints?' asked the Officer-in-Waiting as he inspected dinners. 'Sir!' 'What is your complaint?' 'I found a fag-end in my stew' 'Well, what do you expect – a packet of twenty?'

It was a hard life, but the 'guardsmen' passed out proud people and knew they were the better for their training.

For my part it was a rich experience in which I received nothing but encouragement from all ranks. Our 'parade services', which were 'voluntary', sometimes left the Depot short of fatigue personnel, but the services were real, the prayers reverent, the Regimental Bands inspiring and pulpit opportunities worth everything that could be put into them.

The Commandant, Jim Windsor Lewis, had a young family and the eldest was a girl aged about 5 years or thereabouts, full of life and vigour. She discovered that to get hold of her father's hat, as the family sat in the front pew in chapel on Sundays, and to put it on was entertaining to others, and even more so as she and her nanny competed for possession of the hat. Her father came forward to read the lesson and I was able to slip a note into his hand for I saw he was concerned about family indiscipline. It was wintry weather and in my vestry, not far from the Commandant's pew, was a live fire which made the room comfortable. My note to the Commandant read 'If "X" proves difficult there is a fire in the vestry, nanny could take her there'. He was on tension and announced the lesson 'Here beginneth the twenty-eighth chapter of the book of the prophet Matthew' and he proceeded to read about Mary 'Maudlin'. The lesson being over he glanced at the note I had given him and reaching his pew said 'Fetch the Picquet Officer, there's a fire in the vestry, turn out the fire brigade!' – This cost him some drinks afterwards in the Mess!

Robert was born to our very great delight at this time. Dr Housden, our family friend and doctor, had arranged for Pat's confinement to be in a Wimbledon nursing home and one Saturday night, as we went to bed thoroughly tired, Pat said she hoped nothing would disturb us. An hour later she wakened me. There were signs of Robert's arrival! I rushed her to Wimbledon and in the very early hours Robert arrived. Later that Sunday morning I was due to preach at Holy Trinity Church, Windsor, and the rector – Eric Dawson Walker – welcomed me in choir before the service began 'We are particularly grateful . . . etc . . . for he had a child early this morning only a few hours ago'!

Towards the end of my time in the Depot I was instructed to preach the following Sunday at Sandhurst and I felt embarrassed because the Chaplain General, Freddie Hughes, had more than hinted to me that this was to be my next posting. Was this a trial sermon? I decided I would preach again the sermon that had been on my heart the previous Sunday at Caterham. The subject was when the Lord asked 'Whom do men say that I am?' and how the disciples had had quite a few suggestions *but* when He went on to say 'Whom do you say . . . ' this called for commitment. Certain more senior chaplains discreetly attending the service reported that this was 'hot gospel' and not suitable for Sandhurst . . . I went on promotion to the Canal Zone instead!

I shall always remember the challenging three years I spent at the Guards Depot and the standard of excellence which everybody both exhibited and demanded. Occasionally the NCO in charge of a squad would remain in chapel listening to what was being said. NCOs – who could themselves be hungry for faith – cared for their recruits under training behind all their remoteness of rank and discipline, and often behind a withering rebuke on drill parade there was a degree of humour, although this might not have been recognised at first.

On another occasion I was at fault when Prince Henry, Duke of Gloucester, visited us and all officers had to be in the Officers' Mess to meet him. The order of dress on his departure was 'Battle Dress' with black boots and full turnout of Depot. I had given my battle dress black boots to my gardener! My orderly said he would borrow a pair for me (a guardsman's No.1 pair) which would be perfectly polished and that I might send the boots back by him plus some small thank you. Unfortunately, when the order went out that all ranks would be on parade for HRH's departure my unfortunate guardsman was on a charge for wearing boots not up to scratch. I can't remember what finally was settled, but I had an enormous struggle to protect him The army does not accept excuses, and I was at fault.

My parents were still at Tooting where my father was rector and for some little time we had been anxious about my mother. She had been assured that she did not have cancer, but the family doctor was pointedly discreet. An operation had disclosed her situation inoperable and we knew her death was near. I was under pressure to request cancellation of an overseas posting but this, to me, was not possible. Our doctor was asked to pressurise me but all he did was to ask the date of my posting and tell me that she would have died before then. She was truly a saint, and a courageous one at that, and I felt we had not been fair to her in not sharing with her what almost certainly she already knew. We had set up a bed for her in the drawing room where she had a day and a night nurse and I stretched out on one of the sofas for the last two or three nights. She was more often unconscious than conscious but one night we knew by her breathing that she was 'going'. I stood by her, my hand lightly on her head as she prayed her last conscious words 'Lord, now lettest thou, thy servant, depart in peace, for mine eyes have seen thy salvation'.

It was a death of peace, dignity and lovely faith and a few days later I conducted her funeral service. She was greatly admired and truly loved in the parish and, indeed, by all who knew her, and for her family her loss was profound. She was a saint, but she did not know it. The service was triumphant but I cannot say I found it easy to conduct or to preach at it.

Two days after that Pat and I plus 'Tricia and our baby Robert embarked for Egypt on the *SS Empire Windrush*.

Chapter XI
EGYPT

Some people who knew of the possibility of my going to Sandhurst asked me whether I was disappointed at not going, but frankly I was excited at the prospect of Egypt. It held a breath-taking field of new experience and, perhaps, the possibility of seeing the Holy Land.

We put some of our furniture into store and some we loaned to the chaplain following me at Caterham and we set to to pack crates of more or less standard size, as made available by the army, with all the things we thought necessary. We were to be provided with furnished quarters but these would not include all the things necessary for small children. Our clothes needed to be of a lighter weight and, for me, such books as I would need beyond Bible and prayer book. If there is one thing of which, as a chaplain, one is aware, it is a crying need both of knowledge and wisdom

Advance baggage having been sent ahead by Military Forwarding Office, we ourselves entrained for Southampton, all goods labelled – including 'Tricia! – whom I would never describe as baggage. We found ourselves amongst strangers aboard who soon became friends. The ship's engines broke down in the middle of the Bay of Biscay but this was all part of the journey but soon we were on the move again at eight or ten knots in very pleasant weather and I read the full text of TE Lawrence's *Seven Pillars of Wisdom* to gain some savour of the near East.

The posting spelt promotion for me so that as I arrived in Egypt I became CF (Chaplain to the Forces) 2nd Class once again. The Assistant Chaplain General, Ken Puntan, had written saying that I would go to El Ballah and take charge of the church there as a temporary measure because there had been a serious break-down of a chaplain as charming as he was irresponsible. My area of care was that of Canal North district, Port Said to the north, Tel El Kebir (half way to Cairo) to the west, Ismailia to the south and further south to about halfway to Fayid. HQ Middle East was at Fayid and HQ British Troops Egypt (BTE) was just outside Ismailia at Moascar (Arab word meaning camp). Our quarters at El Ballah consisted of three quite pleasant rooms in a sort of holiday camp set-up. We fed centrally, served by native ser-vants all smartly turned out in their galabeas and coloured head-dress and Pat, who had spent early years in Ceylon, was far more clued up over many things that I was. We needed a car, for she was not entitled to use army transport, and we purchased an almost new Morris at Port Said. When I went to collect this I found we had been gazumped by a higher bidder in Cairo. However, we found a not much older 1.5 litre Riley which looked so smart that it attracted questions as to how I had got it. We were only allowed to take a certain amount of money to Egypt but we were allowed extra for 'leave'. I had had the wit to ask for release of this extra money to buy the car because to have a car was as good as having leave and I could scrape enough for leave from normal army pay. A brigadier on the staff in BTE had the temerity to ask how I got the car and I thought 'silly question, silly answer' and I replied 'Easy! I flogged it out through a Missionary Society'. This nearly got me into trouble!

El Ballah was used as a recreational area because of its bathing facilities on the Canal which were made more interesting with the vast number of seahorses.

The Arabs were as skilled as they were inveterate thieves. One night the local gunner regiment lost a tracked vehicle. There were no track marks left on the sandy road and for quite some time there was no trace of the vehicle. Opposite the Guardroom gate there was a hut made largely of sand blocks as were found almost anywhere in the desert. There would be a doorway and probably one window, but nothing to interest the passer-by. The hut opposite the guardroom gate had simply been built around the missing vehicle!

In due course we moved down to Moascar and had better accommodation on 'The Mall'. Bayswater Road, or 'Red Flannel Alley', was reserved for General Officer Command (General Bobby Erskine) who lived in Flagstaff House, two brigadiers and full colonels. Old Kent Road and the Mall were reserved for Lt.Col. rank. These quarters consisted of four bedrooms and two to three reception rooms with servants' quarters behind. We had a cook, a house-boy (suffragi), and, in the nursery, a nanny. These were totally honest as far as the household was concerned, but woe betide any visitors who thought their belongings were safe *and* woe betide any house-holder who dismissed a servant. Such would know his way round and would not be bound by loyalties.

Pat understood our servants and they were devoted to her. Cooks did local shopping for fresh produce and the remain-der was obtainable by us from NAAFI (Navy Army Air Force Institutes) because no non-military person was allowed to shop there. Cooks would usually expect to 'acquire' from the household larder what they dared for themselves and the other servants. Pat would order what was necessary for the household and instruct that none of this was to be used for the servants, then she would say 'and now what do you want?' (tea, coffee, sugar, etc.). They had ample and more and really appreciated it.

The cooks were proud of their skills and with justification. Birds would arrive on the table looking perfectly shaped but with all bones removed. Sweets would be served often in attractive baskets made of spun sugar. When we entertained, the cook would get the help of his friends and without extra cost to us. Prestige and entertaining walked hand in hand as far as the servants were concerned. Sometimes we ate off our own china in other peoples' houses and General Stopford (commanding 3rd Division) complimented our next door neighbour on his having pleasant china in place of the miser-able issue china we all had! Our neighbour passed on the compliment to us with his thanks!

Moascar Garrison Church was my responsibility and Pat and I loved it. Fifty years later when with Pat in Crowborough I went forward to help a stranger struggling with a walking aid and her letters for post. 'Why', she said 'you are the Neills!' She and her husband, who was on the staff at Fayid, had sometimes worshipped together in Moascar. We had a wonderful Sunday School to which almost all the garrison children came and whose staff included two who went on to be missionaries and two, at least, who were ordained to parochial work at home. Very recently I met a lady lay reader who told me she had found her faith in the Moascar Sunday School and that she had been able to share her faith with her father.

Politically things were not easy. There had been unrest in Ismailia and General Bobby ordered the Lincolns (stationed in Moascar) to march through the city armed and behind their band. They met with nothing but cheering, but political 'authorities' were more than a little critical of such a move.

Rioting in Cairo was largely against King Fouad and a part of the responsibilities of BTE was to look after his safety and maintain order in the city. The king knew this but he also was sensitive to his royal status and dignity. He sent for his War Minister during a particularly ugly time and said 'I hear the British are mustering at Tel El Kebir. If they should move into our capital, how long would it take them?' The reply was, I believe, fifty minutes. 'They are as prepared as that! But if we resist them with our armies, then how long?' 'Fifty five minutes' he replied.

Later, after the abrogation of the Treaty, Cairo did presume to threaten us. The RAF did some diving manoeuvres over their few tanks and dropped a few leaflets. The tanks turned back, apart from one which got bogged down, and BTE received a complaint that the planes had caused unnecessary alarm.

We were having trouble with our elderly church organ during the time leading up to the abrogation of the Treaty. It was unwise/unsafe for our organ-tuner from Cairo to make his routine visits. The organ needed these. It had been a garrison church organ on the Curragh (near Dublin) and now needed constant attention. Our congregation subscribed for a new electronic organ and this I arranged with Comptons. We had three speakers, one in the choir and two positioned skilfully at the west end of the church, high on the stone walls. They were so positioned as to give a suggestion of overtone beat and it was hard to believe that we had not got a new pipe organ.

When this electronic organ arrived it was mistakenly offloaded on to the wrong quay at Port Said and was liable for customs duties which we could not afford. I discovered that the Deputy Chief Customs Officer was a Christian and I drove up to see him 'What do you want me to do?' he asked, 'Absolutely nothing' I replied 'but I would be grateful for advice'. He was most helpful and I was successful. As we talked he told me he was extremely worried. Yesterday, he said that Nahas Pasha had put a bill before the king requiring confiscation of monies from those who had been involved in illegal cotton trade between certain dates. This would have relieved Nahas of bitter rivals. The king had said 'Excellent' but he altered the dates to include Nahas' irregularities. This meant an immediate struggle for power between Nahas and the king. Nahas, the customs officer said, must gain immediate popularity or go down, and probably he would abrogate the treaty within twenty-four hours. He did.

The old organ we gave to the English Church in Amman

and through the generosity of regiments I found volunteers who had had organ building experience who would disman-tle and pack the instrument ready for flight to Amman. In due course the flat trucks arrived, driven by Arab drivers, and set off for the Fayid air station. I had a niggle of anxiety half an hour later and climbed into my car to go to see if they had arrived safely at the air station. They were expected, but had not arrived. I drove on down the road past the airport and about five miles further south there they were, neatly piled in a ditch awaiting local collection, ie theft.

Things were, however, ugly after the abrogation of the Treaty. The Cairo British Club (the Turf Club) was raided and set on fire. Some of the residents lost their lives, some were deliberately disfigured – even dismembered – some were thrown back in the flames. On the Canal Zone some who suf-fered death were so disfigured as to be beyond recognition, but this was due to Cairo thugs rather than to trained Egyptian soldiers.

In Moascar itself we all were within a guarded perimeter, so that apart from the loss of some household servants, clerks and other native employees we did not suffer much. Many domestic servants took risks and stayed. Going about one's normal duties outside could be dangerous and our engineers built a wonderful temporary road in a matter of a few weeks all the way from Moascar to Tel el Kebir, our main store depot. Our faithful cook was arrested trying, without our knowl-edge, to bring us fresh vegetables from Ismailia. We thought he had decided to go home to Upper Egypt but after some months I got a call from the Guard Gate saying an Egyptian was there who maintained he was our cook. He had been in prison in Cairo and had returned to us – it was tear jerking. When finally we left on home posting; he was found weeping outside our gate 'My lady has gone, she couldn't take me'.

During the time of the troubles if we wished to leave the Garrison we had to have an armed soldier in the car, rifle at the ready, for protection – and the paint on the car suffered from the metal of the rifle resting on it. Children who lived outside the Garrison had to be carried to and from school in an army lorry, again with guards at the ready.

The Garrison Church at Moascar had been built by the Royal Engineers and was one of their triumphs. It exactly fitted our needs in simple dignity, high quality of construction and furnishings. Choir surplices disappeared one day, but were later recognised as apron protection in the barber's saloon which the WRAC favoured. There was a splendid Persian carpet (Shiraz) which exactly fitted the spacious chancel floor between the choir stalls but, horror of horrors, my orderly told me one morning 'I've given that old carpet a hair cut' – he had cut off the fringes! There was an occasion when I was privileged to baptise two Mauritian soldiers at evensong. They had been carefully but not fully prepared in their own country and had become the charge of the Garrison Chaplain, Bill Williams. I shall always remember the significance as I took them by the hand saying Achmud (who was one of them) I baptise you John. The Christian name was indeed significant.

We, of course, had weddings also and one non-wedding remains in my mind – 'Padre, what did Corporal X come to see you about?' asked my orderly/verger, 'That is not for you to ask. Why did you ask?' 'Because he is already married!'

Later I rang the company Office and innocently asked if Corporal X was married. 'No' the Company clerk answered 'he has not allocated any marriage allowance'. 'I'd be grateful if you would check with the police at home.' He *was* married and both he and his new-found fiancée were furious with me.

One wedding interview went adrift because the hopeful couple came on the wrong evening and I was not there! Their officer (Captain Allen, WRAC) was a regular worshipper and used to love it when, on occasions in Matins, I would jump straight from the versicle 'Praise ye the Lord' – 'The Lord's Name be praised' to the Te Deum 'We praise thee O God'. She thought it was I who was at fault over this marriage interview and she sent me an Army Charge Sheet (AFB 252). The charge was 'Failing to co-operate with Cupid' and the punishment awarded was five Te Deums. She was cautious not actually to sign the charge sheet herself!

Earlier I mentioned that I had not been posted to Sandhurst. Its Commandant had since taken over command of 3rd Division and was by this time in the desert, north of Moascar. His senior chaplain came to me saying that his GOC had told him that he would attach himself to Moascar Garrison Church. Another of the then Sandhurst staff had arrived in Moascar as Brigadier A/Q of BTE and he, now a regular worshipper in the Garrison Church, asked me 'Why did you not come to us as Chaplain at Sandhurst?' I had thought it was they who had turned me down for having preached a 'hot gospel' sermon!

We had a 'military prison' set up in the desert and one day a call came 'would I help in regard to an impossible prisoner'.

He had been having visions in which he was told that military pursuits were evil and that uniform was not to be worn. This he took seriously and although the temperature of the desert did not make nakedness uncomfortable, it made an awkwardness when a blanket was the only covering he would wear. It was, of course, an army issue blanket! I was allowed to take him outside the prison and we walked the roadway for a considerable time. How we resolved the problem I can't remember, but at least he was not courtmartialled.

Another call was to visit a unit temporarily out in the desert south of Moascar. Morale had dropped and the Commanding Officer was very concerned. When I got there a large group of 'Other Ranks' was assembled in a marquee and I noticed that the NCOs and older 'sweats' had got the only sprung chairs at the back, all the other men were perched on 'chairs, folding, flat'. I walked into the marquee and said 'Good morning gentlemen' then I walked on through the rows of the chairs and said 'will you please turn your chairs round!' There was a whoop of delight from those on the hard chairs and I think everyone – even the soft-seated – sensed the humour of the situation! Soldiers' humour is a prominent constituent of army life but sometimes it can cause embarrassment. The Bishop of London, Dr. Winnington Ingram, once chose to talk to the Grenadier Guards on physical fitness and hygiene. A guardsman knows more about this than most people, despite the then primitive ablution lines at Windsor. The bishop's subject could have been better chosen. 'You know, men, that cold baths are of immense value (they seldom had the luxury of a bath). I take a cold bath two, three or more times a day and it's a wonderful thing to towel oneself down and feel rosy all over' – 'And what does Rosie have to say about it' came a challenging voice from the back.

The one thing I had hoped for became possible – a visit to the Holy Land. The normal route was impossible because of the tensions between Egypt and Israel, so I arranged with a coaling ship company that they would take my car from Suez to Aqaba. Pat had a sister at Fayid who was married to Brigadier Arthur Dove, Chief of Staff to General Robertson, and we made a party of four. Arthur had served in Palestine before the war and this was of great value to our visit and particularly to our journeying across the desert. General Bobby Erskine had asked that I would make notes of the route in the event of his possibly doing a desert exercise.

To Palestine across the Desert of Trans Jordania

To travel through Israel was not possible from Egypt. The Qantara–Gaza route was closed as a result of the Israeli – Egyptian war; and, even if one had been able to travel the Qantara–Gaza route one would not be allowed to enter the old city of Jerusalem from Israeli territory. Furthermore, to travel in or through Israel would mean that the civil authorities in Egypt would not permit the traveller to return to their country – a complication as regards reporting back to duty on the correct date! Our route had to be through Trans Jordania.

We were faced with a choice. We could fly to Mafraq and thence to Amman which would prove an unduly expensive journey, not only because of the cost of air passages but also because of the enormous expenses of taxis etc. when we got there. The other choice was to drive to Suez and embark with our car for Aqaba (the Ezion Geber of the Old Testament where King Solomon kept his fleet and worked his copper mines) and thence to hazard the desert routes.

The car was a 1.5 litre Riley of 1947 vintage and hardly designed – one might say – to forsake the highways for uncertain wadis, boulder tracks, soft sand and open desert. Indeed, Messrs Legrand Bardou of Port Said, from whom I had bought the car, were very cautious in recommending the venture. They suggested that spare torsion bars, towropes, and other gloomy provisions might not be out of place.

We travelled four up. My wife and I, also my wife's sister and her husband who was stationed at GHQ, MELF. Our ration of luggage consisted of one light suitcase per person, a valise containing two blankets or coats per person, sheets, pillows, four safari camp beds, a one gallon thermos container, four chuggles (canvas one-gallon water bottles, self cooling by evaporation), emergency food rations for two days and, of course, the necessary maps and guide books. A roof carrier had been fixed to the car and altogether we made up a formidable load.

Our sea journey was on the *SS Empire Chubb* where we laid out our bedding each night on the deck of the coaling ship, but were given the use of the Captain's cabin during the day. Captain Mackay bade us farewell at Aqaba at noon on Wednesday, 11 July 1951. There was something enigmatical about his cordial and friendly send-off. Perhaps it was tolerance for our foolish optimism, perhaps it was sympathy for our likely sufferings, for there was no shade if the car broke down and desert temperatures in July varied from 110–140°F (40–60°C) for the better part of the day and could freeze at night.

The 1st Royal Lincoln Regiment was stationed at Aqaba and they, too, sped us on our way. It was they who loaned us the chuggles, who supplemented our maps and – perhaps – our apprehension of the journey. But they did more. They sent us off knowing that we were far from friendless should we find ourselves stranded anywhere within their range.

Everything then being in order, including our even having to instruct the immigration authorities where to stamp our passports and our Carnet de Passage, we finally wormed our way through the Lincoln's road block on the Ma'an road at 1.30 PM.

The going was excellent. The road was tarmac and we entered the wadi in high hopes. Had the Children of Israel come this way? Almost certainly it was in this region that they had 'complained of the way' many centuries before – but then they had had no tarmac road, and neither had the Riley motor company begun producing motor cars!

True, our entry into the wadi was in the company of high hopes; but soon these hopes were to become almost as broken as the tarmac. Broken road foundations lay to either side and quietly and grimly lower gears came into play. Would we clear that rock? Was that hump too high? Would the overhung back of the car foul as we navigated that hollow? These questions were to be our constant companions, and at times perhaps to cloud the high spirits in the car.

Another question concerned exactly what damage might result from a misjudgement of driving. The rear shock absorber on the near side was improperly mounted and likely to spring loose on any major bump, the sump was probably stout enough to sustain and survive any reasonable knocks, but the bottom knocked out of the silencer would not contribute to greater comfort, nor a penetration of the petrol tank to any greater speed!

The mountains towered on either side clothed only with the haze of burning heat. There was no sound, no sign of life. Perhaps the Israelites were not unreasonable after all!

It was with a sigh of relief that we regained the tarmac and knew that the worst of the wadi was over. In any case, we were ready for our lunch and were unusually thirsty, a thirst shared but in lesser measure by the car. On our left was a twenty to thirty foot rock face – the wall cut by years of winter rain floods – and there we found shade.

Hopes rose as the water level of the chuggles lowered. The car was not boiling, indeed not even really thirsty. It had come through its ordeal with flying colours. We were some thousands of feet up and sure, we thought, the roads ahead could not be worse.

How little we knew! We could not know then that less than a fortnight later we would be on the same road unharmed – except for a roaring exhaust – looking for our first lunch halt *and* for the 'frightful bits of road' on a route which now seemed almost elementary to negotiate.

Our goal was to reach the Wadi Musa – the Wadi of Moses – so named because it is extremely doubtful whether Moses ever saw the place and much less likely ever struck the rock there to produce water for the thirsty Israelites. Wadi Musa is very close to Petra and we had planned to stay overnight at its Police Post and to spend the whole of the next day in Petra. So, lunch being over we set off on the next stage of our climb. The car was a joy. Accustomed to travelling up and down the

Suez Canal road, and occasionally to Cairo and back, we wondered how its 12 hp would react to such severe demands. Altogether we climbed 5000 ft in eleven miles without any seeming effort and without overheating.

Trees now made an isolated appearance from time to time, and camels disclosed the presence of Bedouin. The camels got off the road to look at us with their supercilious sneer. This is their natural way of looking, no doubt, but it seemed as though they despised us as they saw how we had to carry our water in, by now, dirt clogged and sanded chuggles.

With the top of the ascent there came into view the most southerly part of the railway laid by the Turks, and so often 'mislaid' by Lawrence of Arabia in later years. The map from here showed the road 'maintained' but not 'metalled'. We wondered why. The banks seemed better maintained than the road, but this possibly because others had not had cause to use them as we had. The ruts were worn so deep that there would be no hope of the car clearing the centre stony rise were the banks not to be called into use. But the road was perhaps maintained in so far as its direction was reasonably clear and we did not have to take our bearing on Venus and bounce over trackless ground with hope and uncertainty competing for the upper hand as was to be the case on the return journey.

We crossed the railway line – one can only suppose that the adjective level refers to the trains part of the crossing – and branched off away from our maintained road which pursued its way to Ma'an. The new road was not shown as maintained and perhaps had benefited thereby, for it seemed very fair going at 15 mph. We wondered if the bumps and hollows of the other road owed their origin to Arab maintenance or Arab traffic.

Dusk had descended before us into the Wadi Musa and darkness joined forces with us at the Police Post.

Imagine a small medieval castle, spotlessly clean, white-washed on the inner walls of its courtyard, a flower bed in the centre with stabling, cooking, sleeping and washing facilities all built into the surrounding walls. Such might be Wadi Musa Police Station. Lanterns were lighted. A table was set by the flowerbed, and together with the police corporal and the cook we sat down to drink mint tea and to eat unripe grapes. It was frugal fare but not frugal hospitality, and even the fare improved when we disentangled some of our rations from the dust of travelling.

We breakfasted shortly before 5.30 AM and left the court-yard to select our mounts for Petra at about 6.0 AM. The selection lacked nothing in numbers but all were alike – 'horses' the locals called them – alike in dirt, in age, in reduced condi-tion and in lack of promise. But it must be recorded to the credit of the guide, horseman and boys that – totally unlike Egypt – during the whole day there was no mention of the word 'baksheesh'.

Petra has been so well described that one can do no more than record one's own emotions – surprise and awe at the towering heights on either side of the incredibly narrow defile approach (the sic), intrigue and respect for the skill of the excavators and builders, frustration at all attempts to recon-struct the city life in its hey-day, and sadness and great inter-est at the superstitions and murders of its high places with their channels of escape for the sacrificial blood. The tints of the rocks were unforgettable and even if we did have a little too much sun, we certainly did not have too much Petra.

Again, we breakfasted early in Wadi Musa Police Station before setting off due north for Amman via Tafelia and Karak. The petrol tank had been almost full leaving Suez and we carried a spare one-gallon can. At Wadi Musa we showed half full and we had been promised that a four-gallon can would be available for us there on the morning of our departure. However, the promise was not to be fulfilled and we had to accept the assurance that petrol would probably be available in Shoebeck, and certainly in Tafeilia.

It was Friday 13! We had noted this laughingly, for none of us was superstitious. But Friday 13 was to cause us no little anxiety.

Shoebeck was soon reached by what the map dignified as a road. The route reminded one of a dry version of the lane along which cows used to come to be milked at a country rectory in Co. Cork where more than one summer holiday had been spent as a child. It was a true track in that it was marked by usage, had well defined edges and maintained direction; but had one lent one's car to any friend in England and seen him drive it down such a track, even without passengers and luggage, one would have had increased blood pressure and perhaps decreased friendship. Nevertheless, it was to be the best road we were to know for many miles.

Shoebeck had no petrol despite a small but well placed sign which one had learned to recognise as the Arabic rendering of 'Shell'.

Tafelia was only about thirty miles farther north and so we were still undismayed. There had been no uncertainty regarding our assurances about Tafelia. At times the road compared with the earlier road south of Shoebeck, but at other times we eased and bumped the car along longing for the 'agonies of the lane'. To a car with a higher road clearance – a Land Rover or truck – the road would not have presented much difficulty, but to us it was different. Had we put our wheels in the deep and well-worn ruts we would have see-sawed where we were on the base of the sump and, probably, the petrol tank. This might have been fun if 'where we were' had been the nursery and we of suitable age, but as it was we were presumably responsible people in the middle of nowhere and many miles from our evening destination of Amman.

Tafelia first came into view as a city set 'on a hill'. It was a steep hill of seemingly a regular conical shape and was built up on all sides by stone and mud Arab houses. Our first cry was petrol or 'benzene' as they preferred to name it. But once again petrol seemed scarce. At last a man said he would show us where it might be purchased, and accordingly climbed on to the edge of the car. One could not help but groan for this added and heavy burden unbalancing our already maximum load, but his good will and our hopes of petrol were not to be lightly sacrificed.

As it turned out, all that they could offer us was extended good will and kerosene, and since the former seemed of uncertain extension and the latter of little value we set off for the Police Post. This was right on the summit and we approached it the wrong way. The ground surface was loose stone, there was no defined roadway, and the gradient was not far short of that of a water shute. It was a short-lived relief to get there for we found it was a new post in the process of being built and that the one we sought was down in the town after all. Driving up was genuinely frightening and the prospect of going down by the same route seemed more than we reasonably fair to expect of a car not equipped to act as a toboggan. However, we were directed a better way and soon found ourselves with an officer of the Arab Legion who spoke excellent English and provided us with equally excellent tea.

Nevertheless, there was no petrol! He summoned the garage proprietors and telephoned the local car owners. The best he could offer us was a possible spare tin on the local magistrate's car, expected back that afternoon.

Karak was 46 miles away with a huge wadi on the way. It was the wadi of the brook Cherith and was probably where the prophet Elijah had been miraculously supplied with food during the country's famine. It was a dip of about 3000 feet to a level of 1500 to 2000 feet above sea level, and a climb to a similar height on the other side of something in the neighbourhood of 5000 feet. The surface was loose or broken natural rock. Hairpin bends rendered the gradient possible but also rendered the going positively filthy. The dust raised by the car was being blown across the hill to envelop us on the next corner. But when the dust did miss us the views were panoramic, and the precipices rather more than interesting.

But we had no petrol!

At Tafelia we had had rather less than a quarter of a tank full showing, and even this was uncertain because it might easily become impossible for the remaining petrol to reach the feed pipe owing to the angle at which the car so often had to travel. Our plan had been to arrange with the police to telephone a taxi owner in Karak and to instruct him to set out to meet us at 5.0 PM, taking with him a four-gallon tin. This left us four hours for the forty-six miles if our petrol held out.

We arrived at Karak at 4.50 PM on what must have been our last drop of petrol. We had done the distance from Suez to Karak – some 300 km – in low gears, representing some thirteen hours engine running time in gruelling conditions and all on thirteen gallons of petrol.

Karak was an impressive city dominated by a fine old Crusader castle. The approach was up a steep and broken hill over an unpleasant hump and on to a superbly surfaced road. We were stopped and checked at the police post in just such a way as one might be stopped entering barracks and then allowed to proceed to get petrol. It seemed to us that there was a lack of friendliness here and we were pointedly told that there was nowhere to put up for the night.

Afterwards I was told that there was in fact an Italian Hospital which would have accommodated us, so the behaviour of the Police Post at Karak consequently seemed doubly odd.

It was nearly 6.0 PM when we got on the road for Amman (the ancient Philadelphia) and we were told it was a four hour journey. This seemed very strange in view of the fact that we had been told the road was metalled all the way and the distance was no more than fifty miles.

To our misery the time had been rightly estimated for, with darkness upon us, it took us four-and-a-half hours and our first damage to the car.

The road was broken and rough to begin with and then gave way to a 'road in the making' which consisted of a narrow levelled track of rough broken stones with a wide soft verge rendered hazardous to a degree by large stones and even boulders lying on its surface. The old track road was still in evidence criss-crossing the new and we soon found its uncertain condition was preferable to the new road.

Away in the distance lay barren hills breaking the skyline and marked with the most extraordinary horizontal striations. For some time one put the appearance of these hills down to eyestrain and tried not to look at them. But as we came nearer we found that the strata were indeed actual and that we were approaching the Wadi Mujib.

The Wadi Mujib can only be described as awesome. It was as though giant floods had cut the hills through countless centuries, leaving long and fearsome cuts in the rock face as the water rushed madly on. But now no more remained but an insignificant stream whose bed we were soon to drive across without there being so much as the sign of a bridge. The banks of the ford were perhaps five or six feet deep and anxiety held sway when we found that the car would not take the very severe initial gradient on the other side and the engine was 'firing' unevenly. My passengers wanted to walk, but instead I re-connected the no.1 plug lead and all was well! – it had become detached.

But the light had gone and the roads were really dangerous. A loose corkscrew track climbing 3000 feet with sheer precipices almost all the way on one side was breathtaking. Occasionally we got on to rock bed which was even more bumpy, but the car never faltered once. Again and again we exclaimed at 12 hp. being able to accomplish so much and determined that the Riley company should be told.

At the top of the wadi we hoped to find a better road and drove on anxiously tracing the headlight's beam. We were not disappointed, although we soon were to find that the next wadi was also to be crossed by unmade roads. There were no views this time, only abysmal darkness as we threaded our way down to another ford where we nearly missed the road.

The track crossed the wadi stream obliquely and this was not easy to see in the dark. There was also a semblance of a track rising at right angles from the stream. However we followed the wheel marks of previous vehicles and hoped the track was right. Even now I am not sure that we were right for after miles of travel on the most trying surfaces we joined a better track heading for Amman. Possibly we followed a 'track in the making' for cuttings were visible from time to time and once we sank to sump level in soft sand.

However the Amman track soon became a metalled road and with sighs of relief we were able to engage top gear and make good headway.

It seems that the townships in Trans Jordania were responsible for the upkeep of their own roads and that the Government was responsible only for the main roads. This was to account for our losing our way in the dark in Wadi El Wala and later for the only damage to the car as we entered Amman.

It was nearly 10.30 PM as we entered Amman and we were travelling somewhere between eighty and a hundred kilometres an hour when suddenly we dropped on to an unmade track on the outskirts of Amman. The shock was far beyond all reasonable demands on any car and the lower near side suspension bar – previously distorted in unloading from the ship – snapped in two. Also the neck of the oil filter somehow took the shock and had later to be welded along with the lower front suspension bar. But we had reached Amman!

When we berthed at Aqaba we were met by Colonel Alec Salmon who was a friend of Arthur's and was Chief of Staff to Glubb Pasha. Alec and his wife, Jean, became lasting friends of ours too. When at last we reached Jerusalem Alec Salmon detailed an Arab Legion Sergeant who knew Jerusalem well to care for us and frequently we were the only visible Christian pilgrims in sight. Galilee was not available to us but we drove round and about searching out all we could in the Jerusalem and Samaria area and always met with kindly Arab interest. The Temple Mount on which is the Dome of the Rock and Mosque of El Aksa was explored at leisure, also the Church of the Holy Sepulchre and the town of Bethlehem in which is the Church of the Nativity. We visited Bethany, also Samaria, Sebastia and Jacob's Well where they were beginning to build a church around the latter. While in Bethlehem we were browsing in a shop alongside the church when a young Arab man came hurrying in. I had a flat tyre, might he pump it up for me? I thanked him. He returned asking for the keys of the car so that he could get at my tools, but I told him to get the help of a nearby garage. When we returned to the car all was well and he and his friends asked for *baksheesh*, but I replied 'Nonsense, don't ever let people's tyres down again'. There was a huge laugh at the man's expense who, of course, had never let the tyre down in the first instance.

We found our time in the Garden of Gethsemane very moving and were deeply impressed with the Garden Tomb which exactly fits the Bible story. It was while we were there that we heard small-arms fire and heard people running through the streets calling 'Curfew, curfew'. King Abdullah had been shot as he entered the Mosque of El Aksa.

A week or so earlier he had dined with a number of his senior sheiks and had taunted them with their lack of initiative in regard to relationships between the Arabs and the Jews. He told them how he had used an unmarked car to travel across the Jordan and how he had held discussions with Ben Gurion and other of Israel's leaders and that their discussions and hopes were acceptable in the UK and America. Colonel Salmon told me he had asked General Glubb what he thought of the King's disclosures, for they both had been at the dinner. Glubb replied 'I give him a week to live'.

We were given a special pass to leave Jerusalem for our army leave was running short and we had the desert journey before us. We were thoroughly searched by the Legion soldiery as we left Jerusalem and we set off to stay overnight at Amman. As we drove down towards Jericho the road was blocked by crowding and demonstrating desert Arabs. Suddenly I realised the reason why so many vehicles we had encountered on the road had broken windscreens and windows. I was horrified. I had Pat and her sister, two very beautiful people in the car and anything could happen. I prayed silently and anxiously and felt that I should not try anything dramatic. So, slowing the car to a standstill I lowered my window and asked what was wrong. 'American?' they shouted in anger and I said 'No, British'. There was a pause before the leader of the gang shouted 'Pass, British'. This happened once again as we rose from the

Allenby Bridge towards Amman, but we felt more assured. The Mufti was in Jerusalem and the Arabs felt that America was behind the King's assassination. Abdullah was known to be specially attached to our King.

We left Amman the following afternoon and set off for Maan, to be within easy reach of Aqaba the next day. I kept my eye on the old disused railway line for the light would soon fail. There was always the risk of soft sand and I took awful risks in not really knowing what was firm and what was not. This meant driving round quite large areas which looked uncertain. The light had now gone. The stars were out and I discovered I had lost the railway. I consulted Arthur quietly as to whether we should stop where we were so that with sunrise we would be sure of our direction. He asked how long did I think we had been travelling and what I estimated would have been our average speed. Then he said 'Follow towards that star and we should see the lights of Maan in about twenty minutes'. Thank God we did.

Back again in Egypt

It was while we were in Egypt that the King (George VI) died and none of us will ever forget how Egyptians stopped us in the street to say how truly sorry they were. We all suffered a deep sense of loss and at one service I took on the edge of the Canal I saw tears from a Sergeant Major as we sang the National Anthem. How cross I was with the press when one of them crawled into the parade to photograph him.

The time had come to leave Egypt's Canal Zone. We had much to remember; leave periods in the Holy Land and in

Cyprus; incredible mirages regularly seen of motor transport where there were no roads on early morning at El Kirsch; ships but yards away across the sand, journeying up and down the Canal between Port Said and Ismailia; and our driving up and down the Canal Road which lay between the Canal itself and the filthy 'sweet water canal'.

We had contacts with the Church Missionary Hospital (CMS Hospital) at Shebbeen near Cairo as well as with the CMJ (Church Mission to the Jews) School at Faggala in Cairo itself. Egyptian students' political unrest was sometimes in evidence. One class had draped the teacher's rostrum with the Union Jack so that he would have to tread on it. The next day that teacher was confronted with 'EVACUATION' in large letters on the blackboard. The third day the board read 'EVACUATION WITH BLOOD' and the atmosphere was tense until the teacher added 'DYSENTRY'.

It was good to be returning to the homeland, but it was wonderful to have had the experience of an Egyptian posting.

Chapter XII

FIVE YEARS IN ENGLAND

Patricia was now an intelligent little girl and Robert, too, was far from lacking although only just over three years of age. We all enjoyed the journey home on the *SS Dilwara*, stopping briefly as we did at Malta and Gibraltar where Pat and I had a chance to see something of the sights. I was the only chaplain aboard and I used the forward 'cabin' next to the anchor locker as a place where people could see me with any problems. This was somewhat airless and subject to exaggerated movement when the sea became disturbed and I enjoyed getting back to the family when my two-hour stints were over.

The Navy had generously taken our Riley home for us but it was a bit of a wreck when they picked it up at Port Said. I had left it a day in advance because they wanted it on a Sunday. Arab acquisitiveness had left the car in a sorry state so that when we got home I had the car waiting for me together with a sizeable bill from a reliable garage.

My mother had died before our going abroad and my father, too, had died nearly a year before we returned. Pat's parents had moved to Crowborough and it was to them we went to enjoy the chill of high altitude after three years of exhausting desert heat. Leave in the army was never an entitlement and I found myself, almost without any leave, posted to Catterick in North Yorkshire on Good Friday as DACG Northumbrian District. Here were the training regiments for the Cavalry as well as for the Royal Signals. There were two Garrison Churches, St. Oswald's which was the District HQs church, and St Aidans which was used by the Royal Corps of Signals, and these were regularly well filled and had full programmes of activity. I was allowed a colleague and, for part of my time, a second assistant in his early training. This latter was a fine scholar, fearless in splendid preaching, but very shy in social contact. His deep sincerity was recognised and because of this he escaped censure in a pulpit attack he made on what he considered to be the purposeless idleness of troopers, NCOs and Officers of the Regiment in Church. When he had well nigh reached the limit of tolerance he ended his sermon abruptly with the words 'And for what we have received may the Lord make us truly thankful'. I was not in church that morning but was preaching elsewhere and I was glad! The DACG duties included liaison with the many Territorial Army chaplains over a wide area and I was kept hard occupied in very pleasant surroundings. Both children went to Frenchgate School in Richmond and in regard to this Pat joined with other 'mums' in ferrying some children to and fro.

The senior of my colleagues was of very high church tradition and felt restricted by the 'centrality' of army worship so, once a month, I used to give him a Sunday morning off duty so that he could go and enjoy his 'holy smoke' in some church within reach. The Chaplain at St. Aidans ranked as CF 3rd class and 'ran his own show' excellently, but there was something about him which disturbed him that people could not understand. Poor fellow, his widowed mother-in-law had settled herself on him and she had decided she was in love with him.

Duty took us to London at times and on one occasion we found ourselves travelling first class on the same train as Michael Ramsay, then Archbishop of York. He was travelling second class Pullman (a now non-existent luxury service) and we, on warrant were travelling first class. We chaplains tried not to let him see us entrain!

Pat was not well and this worried me. Was it the sharp air after Egypt, where she had also been very unwell, or was it perhaps that while there we had regularly drunk fresh lime juice, not knowing it was supposed to thin the blood? Her blood count was wrong and then she developed a form of thrombosis in her upper leg which required immobility in bed for some weeks. I set up a bed in my study, but was very worried when the doctor told me I had risked her life in carrying her downstairs. Thank God all was well and she was still able to be part of our work, even on the telephone.

Parade services had, by now, been abolished and soldiers were no longer entitled to transport to church from outlying camps, nor were we entitled to the richness of bands leading the singing. Junior recruits of two of the Cavalry training regiments were unable to come to church and I made a plea to the Brigadier, making the point that the first four to six weeks in a soldier's life were compellingly formative and that a recruit could well adopt an amoral or Christless attitude during those weeks which could colour the whole of his career. Of course no 'trooper' was permitted to be seen in his uniform until he could wear his regimental insignia with smartness and dignity – the redcaps (Royal Military Police) would see to that. Would the Brigadier gain permission to authorise transport and I would reserve special seats in the church? The Brigadier rang me up a few days later 'Mohammed could not come to the mountain, but would the mountain come to Mohammed?' We managed to fit in a short Sunday service in the regimental lines, a service which the Brigadier himself frequently attended.

Catterick, however, was to prove one of our shortest postings, only seven months. Pat went home to her parents in Crowborough for she was still under par, Robert went with her, but poor 'Tricia had to be farmed out until the end of term when she, too, travelled down to Crowborough. I stayed on some weeks, living finally in the Officers' Club. Just before this I had agreed the purchase of a Highland pony which I thought might help Pat in her recovery, but the pony proved to be in foal and we were able to delay acceptance of it until after we had been re-housed at my new appointment.

The Chaplain General (Victor Pike) had called me down to see him and taken my breath away by telling me I was to be the new Warden of the Chaplains' Training Centre and Depot at Bagshot Park, and there I was for three and a half years. This was, perhaps, the most wonderful job in the Department with enormous potential for spiritual ministry and evangelism right across the army. We had special courses for Territorial chaplains and sometimes retiring officers. The

Officers' Christian Union – a strong evangelical body amongst whom I numbered myself – approached me for special facilities at Bagshot, but I had to explain that the width of our remit was wider than their contribution and that they would have to fall into line. This they fully understood but later, when as Chaplain General I asked them further to fall into line so that they could be fully recognised in all three Services and be members of the Council of Voluntary War Workers (CVWW), there was determined initial resistance from the Plymouth Brethren membership of their council, some few of whom resigned.

The training of chaplains at Bagshot did not seek to standardise the spiritual life of the chaplains, but attempted to make them fully aware of the opportunities and challenge which lay ahead of them. We shared devotional discussion, lectures and worship together. Our task at Bagshot where I was privileged to be double-banked with two outstanding chaplains for most of my time (Dr David Hutchinson Whiteford, Church of Scotland as Deputy Warden, and Patrick Renison, Church of England as Chaplain) was to familiarise chaplains with army procedures so that they could fit in and work within what would be, for them, a new sphere of ministry. They would be as exposed as a goldfish in its bowl and it was more than their spiritual integrity that would be exposed.

The most frequently conducted courses, some for officers, some for senior non-commissioned officers and many for 'other ranks' were designated 'Christian Leadership Courses' but they really were Christian discipleship courses. Who can lead unless he is himself a disciple? Free discussion was a most valuable element in these courses and an enrichment also to us chaplains.

The proportionate number of chaplains for each religious denomination in the army was carefully watched and I remember one chaplains' course when a delightful young rabbi joined us. He was naturally concerned about what foods he could eat and to avoid complications he told our Admin. Officer that he was a vegetarian. 'Did it matter?' 'No' said Lt. Col. Irvine 'we have three on the staff already' 'Among the chaplains?' 'No, the warden's ponies!' He was fortunate that the rabbi, too, had a keen sense of humour.

The pony that I had purchased from Scotland to help Pat in her recovery had proved fit to travel and she presented us with the most beautiful foal which later was to take third prize at the Windsor Show. We added an Irish chestnut of 16.2 hands and Seamus (Irish) and Calleagh and Liam were well known. A friend, Colonel Mike Whistler hunted with Seamus, but we merely used the animals for hacking. Seamus was not really fully trained and of course, we had to break in Liam from the start. We had permission to ride out from Bagshot into Windsor Great Park and when Liam was ready for it we backed him with a filled sack. He progressed from being led by a rein to being allowed to run free and coming to the call like a dog and in due time 'Tricia rode him and found him extremely responsive. Sometimes she rode Calleagh on her own and just occasionally the pony felt she had had enough and would go no further . . . I used to say she had run out of petrol. Seamus was high spirited but I think all three ponies were as fond of us as we were of them. Not so, others! We had two troopers on a course from the Household Cavalry at Windsor. 'Might we be allowed to ride' they asked 'the luxury of a civilian saddle is tempting'. Pat took them down to the animals and the troopers, with Pat present, saddled them. They enjoyed their ride, cleaned and returned the tack and we were pleased about their responsible behaviour. After prayers the next evening they thought they might ride again, without permission and bare back. The first to mount was thrown straight off, the second mockingly mounted and was whirled away at full pace to the electric fence. The trooper threw himself off – at least he said so! – as Seamus came to a sudden stand-still by the wire. A senior RAF officer called one afternoon and asked, as we were having tea, if he might ride Seamus. Pat told him gently that he was too heavy for 6.2 hands, but he persisted. 'All right,' she said 'but just in the paddock and *no* jumping'. He rode round a few times, Seamus was a lovely animal to ride, and the Air Vice-Marshal succumbed to the temptation of a jump. Seamus took him over the jump and set off at once for a large rhododendron bush and put him in the middle of it. We hated parting with them when we knew our time at Bagshot must be coming to an end, and we took the greatest care to find them new homes. A delightful sergeant major, ex Cavalry, who was farming in Kent wanted Calleagh for his wife to ride but I was not prepared to part the two – mother and foal. Late that evening he rang back from Kent 'would I accept an offer if he agreed to take Liam?' I replied that I was selling them very much below their value because we wanted good homes for them, not money. He replied that if I had upped the price he still would have to agree because his daughter had prayed as she went to bed that the Lord would let her have the pony. Seamus was bought for Mrs Oppenheimer where he would have very special care as her personal horse.

Bagshot, however, was far more than horse and ponies. It was a place where men, and WRAC too, found faith or, more truly, where the dear Lord found them and where, as one young officer put it, God had driven the first nail into the coffin of his disbelief.

For me it also meant a closer touch with the 'home church' as we called upon its excellence for special courses and for the conduct of 'quiet days'. Not normally functioning over the weekends, I found myself in civilian churches and frequently one felt oneself unworthy to be the preacher. There came a Trinity Sunday when I preached in the presence of Her Majesty at Windsor. Other daunting occasions were at Westminster Abbey (Evensong) and Matins at St. Paul's Cathedral. But it is not numbers or prestige of pulpit which matter most to the preacher, it is that – as St. Paul put it –he might be given utterance to preach the Word boldly. How often I dared to remind my God of what he had said to Moses 'Have not I made the mouth'.

My first appearance on television was in connection with our ministry to people doing their National Service and I had in support two young people who had finished their National Service and were now in responsible jobs, and who still thanked God for Bagshot. After a later TV appearance 'Tricia said 'Daddy, why did you gulp before coming alive on the screen?' I didn't know that I had, but I told her that it surprised me to see that the back of the head on the monitoring screen was my own head!

It was with great sadness that I handed over the work at

Bagshot to my successor who, sadly, was soon to die in office. We had, as living quarters, the suite of rooms which had been Prince Arthur's. Lady Patricia Ramsay (whose father was the Duke of Connaught and had received the house as a wedding present from his mother Queen Victoria) visited us more than once and encouraged us by saying that she was confident that her parents would truly be glad their house was cared for and used as the Army was using it. The main house still had some of her furniture loaned to the Department including a most beautiful portrait of her which finally had to go to her regiment in Canada. Our official visitors who graced the house from time to time – many of them more than once – included the Archbishop of Canterbury (Lord Fisher) and his wife; Lord Coggan, before he became a bishop, conducted a quiet day for us; Dr. William Barclay, the well known biblical commentator, was also a frequent visitor and there were many other men of God whom I have not mentioned who contributed to the Christian richness of the work entrusted to us.

Chapter XIII
PARIS

One would normally expect such a posting as Bagshot to last three years and Pat and I had decided to be ready then for a new posting as far as family and domestic ties were concerned. We sold the ponies. 'Tricia had outgrown her prep school, Elmhurst School in Camberley, and the time had come for her to enter the Royal School at Bath. Robert had been at the kindergarten of Elmhurst but we decided we must get him 'settled' in schooling before we found ourselves possibly – we guessed – in the Far East. We were very grateful to Ted and Beth Aldrich-Blake, who accepted Robert early at Earleywood, Ascot.

The posting came and it was to Supreme Headquarters Allied Powers Europe (SHAPE) then stationed just outside Paris. I was to be senior chaplain with no jurisdiction over other nation's chaplains, but just to ensure that everything worked smoothly and to undertake myself responsibility for all Anglican chaplaincy work. I held higher rank than the rank of the other chaplains but this, I hope, bothered no-body. The church building was a large and plain auditorium with a series of chaplains' vestry/offices opening off a long side corridor with a choir vestry at the end. I described this chapel as a sort of religious cafeteria on Sundays because in it were held: 7.0 AM RC Mass (sometimes); 8.0 AM Anglican Holy Communion; 9.30 AM RC Mass; 11.0 AM Anglican Matins; 12.0 PM Methodist Worship; and 2.30 PM Lutheran Worship. The only time there was embarrassment had to do with the parking of cars. Traditionally, parking restrictions were waived near the church on Sunday mornings, but on one Sunday the Military Police unfortunately decided to 'book' the owners of the cars – but only during the Methodist service! This disclosed a sensitivity which soon was happily sorted out. I was fortunate indeed to inherit a reasonable volunteer choir and for most of my time to have Richard Lloyd (later organist of Durham Cathedral) who was doing his National Service to be our organist and choirmaster. A few of the choir are now ordained and in live ministry as is also a clerk I was apportioned. A replacement clerk I was fortunate to have was Peter Reeve who was the son of the Bishop of Lichfield and is today fully engaged with the service of the Church Commissioners. When I needed a replacement clerk I appointed the staff officer who dealt with such duties and asked for Peter 'Padre, you can't have him, he's working in this office. What would you want him for?' I explained that I was not always in my office and I needed somebody who could handle with understanding the questions which arose so frequently. 'What would young Reeve know about such matters?' He is the son of the Bishop of Lichfield' 'A bishop's son make my morning coffee! You can't have him!' – but of course I did. Peter Reeve's duty had previously been postal clerk.

SHAPE family village, where many families lived, was some distance away and Sunday morning worship on Camp Voluceaux was not convenient for them. The 'village' was centred around a chateau with a very attractive chapel. We had evensong there and it became popular with some of the lads billeted in SHAPE proper to attend this service, but it meant they missed their evening meal. Those who had transport would take the others. Pat said she would handle some sort of refreshments in the house we had rented at L'Etang la Ville on the edge of the Forêt de Marly. During school holidays many Officers' children joined their parents and often came to this service and on to supper at our house. We found that preparing food was becoming too big a problem for Pat, who continued to undertake the dessert. I was allowed to purchase food from the NAAFI and give it to the Army Catering Corps for preparation as substantial cocktail eats. The cooks did marvellously and I would collect trays of 'eats' every Sunday afternoon including Ice Cream Cake – except for one Sunday when somebody managed to collect them before I did!

It was early morning on a bank holiday observed by SHAPE when we were disturbed by a loud banging on our hall door! I was confronted by a group of the 'Sunday evening lads', led by an American Warrant Officer, armed with brushes, buckets, etc. 'We've come to decorate your hall.' The hall was indeed shabby and Pat and I were deeply moved. We managed to get together some food for them despite the bank holiday.

I had been at SHAPE a few months when the Commandant of the British element sent for me 'Padre, I hear you have put in to see the Deputy Supreme Commander (Field Marshal Montgomery). May I know what it is about?' 'No,' I said, 'I'm too old a soldier to say anything which would involve your responsibilities.' 'I know,' he said 'but General Rupert (Cochrane) is very concerned and has told me to find out.' 'For General Rupert's ears and yours only' I said 'I'm concerned that he has not come to church here either in my predecessor's or my time.' Monty was magnificent and despite my, I hope, sensitive reproach he was the first one on the telephone to congratulate me when, a week or so later, I was awarded the OBE. A decoration was the last thing I anticipated. I had been awarded a Mention in Dispatches during the war and had been appointed a Knight Commander of the Order of Orange Nassau (with Swords) by the Dutch after the Nijmegen/Arnhem engagement. I thought that was the last of my decorations. I never saw any of my citations but I believe the OBE came as a result of work at Bagshot.

We loved our time at SHAPE and so had 'Tricia and Robert who had, of course, joined us in the school holidays. We had bought a small caravan for holiday use and we had one delightful holiday going round the chateaux of the Loire and another in the Black Forest before another posting made caravans unnecessary. My daily need of our car (a Humber Hawk) meant that Pat was 'grounded' so I bought a little Fiat Topolina from a Naval officer who was retiring. A great friend who lived in the neighbouring village (Colonel Alec Salmon, afterwards Lord Chancellor's Ecclesiastical

Secretary) used to travel into SHAPE with me when his car was either 'in dock' or needed by his family. Choosing between a Humber Hawk and a baby Fiat, he used to ask 'Are we travelling peerage or steerage?' He had been Chief of Staff to Glubb Pasha and it was when we visited the Holy Land from Egypt that our friendship began.

*We h*ad purchased the Humber Hawk earlier about which there is an amusing story. It had been arranged that Pat would collect it in London and she and 'Tricia both turned up at the appointed time. Pat was expecting to collect a burgundy coloured car with a beige interior, but what was waiting for her was a two-tone car, burgundy and beige. Frantic 'phone calls ensued including one to me in France (a more difficult exercise in those days) and the net result was that we became the proud possessors of a two-tone car. Pat and 'Tricia then set off to Fishguard (Wales) for the ferry to Ireland, collecting Robert from school on the way. The biggest problem arose when they needed to fill the car – where was the petrol cap? The petrol attendant (we always had petrol attendants in those day) looked everywhere and finally Pat had to delve into the car manual to find its whereabouts. There were two petrol caps, each of which was disclosed when the rear reflectors were removed.

My posting to Cyprus came as a total surprise. I received a telephone call at our hired 'quarter' from the Deputy Chaplain General (David Lloyd-Evans) 'I want to be the first to congratulate you. You have been promoted first class and will be appointed Assistant Chaplain General Middle East HQ. The official letter is in the post'. The Middle East HQs had moved from Fayid on the Suez Canal to Episkopi on the southern coast of Cyprus and its jurisdiction covered North Africa, Malta and Aqaba.

SHAPE was to be one of my shortest postings for I had only been there 14 months.

Chapter XIV

CYPRUS

I had come to know Cyprus through visiting it on leave from Egypt in 1951 and 1953. Set in the blue of the Mediterranean it can be poetically described as a jewel of changing colours. The dull sandy and rocky grandeur of its burnt-up summer aspect is broken by the glaring white of the asbestos mines, the rich green of its mountain pine forests and the brilliant copper coloration of some of its inshore waters.

Then comes winter with the mountains topped with glistening snow, the gardens and fruit groves colourful with oranges, lemons and grapefruit, and even water exploring the tracks and river beds dried up and barren from the summer sun.

But it is spring which unfolds its greatest beauty: wild flowers and grass growing where once all looked desert, the Messoori Plain golden with its ripened crops, the fresh green of the vineyards triumphant against the increasing heat of the sun.

This was the Cyprus to which the Army came for peace and

welcome from the unrest of a troubled Egypt and from the dehydration and later animosities of an Egyptian desert. This was the Cyprus famous for its hospitality, and refreshing in its people of integrity.

The roads were narrow and breathtaking both in the quality of their views and in the hazards of their traffic. A camel train, or a narrow gauge railway, or a stream of horn-sounding cars – it mattered not at all. Cyprus was dignified with marks of its ancient history and a fussy mortal was only a transitory visitor.

Now six years later there was anxiety afoot. Most of the village mayors had joined the quietly growing Communist party. The new Archbishop, who had taken his name from the ancient appellation of the country – Makarios – was wedded to union between the Greek influenced Church and Greece; and the Turks – survivors of the occupation forces of the proud and ancient Ottoman Empire – were watching anxiously both these dangers to their peace and security.

How soon all was to change! Sinister propaganda, infusions of hate into the youth, reckless abandon of her qualities of courtesy and patience, all these bred a new generation resentful of British rule and forgetful of the vast improvements in health, hygiene, agriculture, water supply and roads which had been brought about within that period. Cyprus had never known self-rule and now she was to grasp it. Romans, Venetians, Turks and others had held her reins of government in the past, but now a change to self-rule captured the imagination.

During the days of Ottoman rule the Orthodox Church had looked to its clergy for assurance of religious and political freedom. Preferment was given to those clergy who best could ensure the safety of their people. Gradually political prowess was recognised as part of the priestly role, and finally the call to *Enosis* and *Eoka* became the call of the Cypriot Church. Her priests were supplied with anti-British slogans and banners to display in their churches, and sermons were supplied to them with instructions when they should be preached. The church bell rang for more than religious worship: it rang for political meetings, for anti-British demonstrations, and on more than one occasion to gather its people to come to jeer at British funerals nearing their cemeteries.

Cyprus had changed. And yet it was not Cyprus – rather there had been sown upon it tares where once was there was wheat.

Chaos had hurt all and helped none. Working formulae had been devised to hold together in one the richness of so many traditions. But the evil of implanting hate and intolerance in a child's heart had nevertheless been committed. Ambition and force had been bound together in the thinking processes of youth. The roads were strewn with party names even as the buildings were likewise disfigured and road markings rendered illegible. Signposts had been bent and disfigured so that they no longer pointed the correct way. All this seems full of significance. Reality was endangered from the hands of those trusted to guide. The new Cyprus – will it rush into chaos, anarchy and confusion, or will it emerge the 'Blessed Isle' which once indeed was its name.

Cyprus was not yet a divided island and parts of it were distinctly ill at ease. The Greeks were openly hostile to the Turks and vice versa. 'Incidents' were frequent and British influence was unwelcome. Officers and other ranks were at all times armed outside barracks and families had been sent home except for such as were fortunate enough to live in protected family camps. The terrorist activity was mean and nasty. A decent Cypriot might find a paper slipped under his door which would read something like this (and I quote from memory) 'You will find among the vegetables outside XXX shop in Limassol in XXX Street and under the fruit in a certain display basket a gun. You will take this unseen, shoot a British officer, and return the gun to be hidden . . . Failure to do this will ensure a death in your family'.

On arrival in Cyprus I was dismayed to find some chaplains were carrying handguns and horrified – just before my arrival – to hear of a chaplain being forcibly relieved of his gun when relaxing by the seaside. Guns for chaplains were at once disallowed, but I found myself at variance with General Ken Darling, who commanded the Parachutes. He 'required' his chaplains to carry arms. Finally he graciously gave way.

Chaplains went out on duties with an armed soldier escort but when I could I drove my own little private car, a small Standard, and I did not wear uniform until arrival at my destination. Nevertheless, there were places where army transport and full armoured car protection was enjoined. On one occasion, rounding a hilltop in my little car, there was a heavy burst of fire ahead. I drove on cautiously hoping that the firing was not ranging on the road. There was another burst, a pause, and yet another burst, but I discovered to my relief it was only a military firing range in active use.

The situation, however, had improved and wives including Pat were coming out. We had been to Cyprus on leave twice when previously we had been serving in the Canal Zone and then the beauty of the island had captivated us. The heights near Troodos were joy and peace then, but not now as secure. A Welsh regiment displayed its humour nevertheless, and on the rocks bordering dangerous and very hilly hairpin bends one would often see 'Home Rule for Wales' written in large letters.

When Pat arrived I had no entitlement to married quarters at Paramali in Episkopi and we moved into a holding camp at Berengaria outside Limassol which was sparsely furnished. As Pat jumped into bed the first night I heard her exclaim 'Ouch, this is board and lodging'.

Work on the island was challenging, but I was somewhat concerned for I felt some of the chaplains had lost something of spiritual urgency. There was an older one who had become regarded as 'bolshy' towards higher command but was in fact one of the best in self-giving, and there was another who was a better rugger referee than a spiritual force. One really concerned me. He was with a Guards regiment, had cut his cap to the shape common in the Regiment and was enjoying the nightlife of the nearby town. There was nothing viciously wrong, but the regimental guardroom had been timing his ins and outs and finally reported him to the adjutant. The DACG (Deputy Assistant Chaplain General) came to me about it because the CO was requesting his removal and sadly his senior chaplain and DACG had not acted before. Mercifully, I knew the CO and we agreed the chaplain's worth as being fundamentally of value despite his being on the slippery slope. We each agreed that we would independently give him the 'rocket' of his life with all possible encouragement at the same time to pull himself together. We would not move him as a failure but I would move him in three months time to a less glamorous posting. We hoped he would leave the Guard's regiment on the crest of the wave rather than out of the trough of failure. Thank God, he really proved his worth. In later years when he was in a very trusted posting, I remarked on his baldness and he said 'You are responsible for that'. I think I was sad but not sorry.

The chaplain at Tripoli had been a prisoner of war with the Japanese and this had had its effect on him. He put in an application for leave asking for more than double the permitted period and saying it was due because of previous circumstances. I granted leave for the normal period and treated his over-application as an amusing 'try-on'. I got a rude letter back and so felt I must go to see him without delay. He and his wife met me at the airport with charming courtesy. We did not mention leave and I visited, with him, all the regiments and units in his care and discovered what a faithful work he was doing. I stayed with them in their quarter for a few days and towards the end, when he was out on duty, I asked his wife if ever he suffered from memories of his POW experience. 'Does he not' she replied and she told me he could not remain or sleep in any room unless windows and door were open. She said that he 'went berserk' if he felt his liberty was being curtailed. I was so glad I had gone to see him.

It was with him, but on another occasion, that we spent a fascinating few hours at Leptus Magna and there I was shown a gruesome grave, recently uncovered, with the skeleton totally distorted. It was the North Wall of the ancient city and I said 'Could he have been crucified?' A doctor had seen the skeleton the day before and had voiced the same idea, although he may not have known the significance of 'outside the north wall'. Leptus Magna was the birthplace of Septimus Severus, who was the Officer Commanding the Roman troops guarding Hadrian's Wall dividing Scotland from England. He was regarded as a very cruel general and was recalled by the Emperor Hadrian (c.140) to undertake the genocide of the Jews in Palestine and the total destruction of Jerusalem.

There was a hut set apart near Beren Garia for the use of a very sincere Army Scripture Reader and an RAF lad had provided it with a notice board

Sunday Services   Church of England . . .
                                   Methodist . . .
                                   United Board . . .

But if you really want to enjoy yourself – it's here . . .

As Assistant Chaplain General I could not have charge of a church with its congregations and this I missed, but my opposite number in the RAF and I were allowed to minister in the HQs church at the senior chaplain's invitation. The RAF Assistant Chaplain-in-Chief was a man of unusually short stature and he caused great mirth one Sunday evening, well nigh lost in the pulpit. His text was 'Hearing a voice but seeing no man'!

Bill Leonard-Morgan, who had been a valued supported in my work at SHAPE, had been posted to MELF on the staff as assistant Garrison Commander under Hugo Pyman, again pulled his weight in the garrison church. Bill's marriage had broken and he had two lively boys. He asked if we would be prepared to have him and the boys to live with us during the school holidays and said he would take them off camping for some of the time. I was dismayed for the boys as I saw the time drawing near for their camping! His excellence as a staff officer obviously did not extend to the nitty gritty of camp life and as Pat and I saw them off taking our Robert with them I said to Pat 'They will be back in the morning' – they were, and camping was abandoned. The second tent didn't erect, the boys were boiled alive on the Pan Handle (the eastern extremity of Cyprus) and many necessary camping utensils were not to hand!

We had been having disturbing reports about Pat's mother who was by now in hospital and I had a strong hunch that she was dying. Pat was very surprised when I told her I had booked her to go home on a plane the next day. 'Tricia – still a school girl – said she would run the house with me and do the cooking (we did have a Turkish maid, but her skills were limited). Pat was met by her sister at the airport telling her she was just too late to see her mother. 'Mater', as I called her, was a very, very great loss for she was the most loveable person. We held on to the Leonard-Morgans for a few days but they could see they were too much for 'Tricia and they managed to find alternative accommodation.

We were unexpectedly adopted by a beautiful young tortoiseshell kitten which was the joy of 'Tricia's heart, but a day or two later there was a shocking howling of a wild, really ugly, cat and our little kitten hid herself under the dining room table, for we were at breakfast. The cat's howling persisted as it cautiously came into the house, to the dining room door, saw what must have been her kitten and summoned it in unmistakable terms. The kitten finally spat defiance and stayed with us. Twice, if not three times, we thought we were going to have to cope with a litter for we had not thought to have it neutered. No litters, fortunately, but we gave it to the paymaster's wife before we returned home on posting. She wrote later to say a litter had arrived.

After but a short time in MELF Pat and I were walking out of church one Sunday morning when I saw Colonel Robert Hornby (Command Public Relations Officer) directing photographers to us 'with intent'! The next day it was announced that I had been appointed Chaplain General. I had written off as impossible remarks by a general and his wife visiting MELF HQs and later by Pat Pirie-Gordon, the Director of the Army Agent's Bank (Glyn Mills) also visiting Cyprus on duty, that I was to be the next Chaplain General. Victor Pike had, however, confirmed this when I was in the UK on the Chaplain General's annual conference. I did not know exactly when – and Pat was the only one I was allowed to tell. Robert Hornby's appearance on the scene was supported by 'You know something I'm not officially allowed to know'. He and I had known each other when he was in charge of Public Relations in Egypt and when I was DACG Canal North.

'Tricia was at school and other girls there saw the announcement of my appointment in the paper before she did. There was a buzz of excitement around her for the Royal School was a school specially catering for officers' daughters. The first telegram of congratulations which I received was from the domestic staff at Bagshot and I appreciated this very greatly.

Chapter XV
CHAPLAIN GENERAL

My appointment as Chaplain-General was an enormous challenge. The short time before I actually took up office I spent 'working hours' in the war office going through files and being alongside Victor Pike as he disentangled himself from CG duties. He was more than encouraging but, at the same time, had a mischievous sense of humour. He did not tell me how he had told the other ACGs personally that each would be the next CG. There was, therefore, some disappointment in the air but all accepted the situation with generous grace. One said he had been 'kicked in the teeth', but his friendship and loyalty were really meaningful and it was he himself who told me of his initial hurt. I was, I think, the junior ACG at the time and at my first meeting in conference with these splendid people I paid tribute to them as heretofore friends and seniors. I said I still respected the dignity of 'The Chair' and would continue to do so, but that I hoped we would continue on Christian name terms on all unofficial occasions. This was often an occasion of mirth when others were not present – 'Sir, are you now CG or are you Ivan?'!

The Chaplains' Department functioned under the Permanent Under Secretary of State for War and Sir Richard Way could not have been more helpful, as was also his deputy, Sir Arthur Drew. Severe criticism of the Department came in from the Far East very shortly before the time of my appointment and General Sir Richard Hull, Commander in Chief, being in London, came and visited me in my office in Berkeley Square. I think he realised that the criticisms were ill-founded and he reassured the Army Council accordingly. Nevertheless, I had to answer to a special committee in regard to chaplaincy policies. Sir Arthur – as Deputy Under Secretary – offered to accompany me and to stand by me were I in danger of being 'torn apart', and this I greatly appreciated. In fact the committee was far from hostile and I had an easy run.

There was a great Centenary Celebration in Croydon at that time to which I was invited to attend and there I encountered Archbishop Fisher for the first time since my appointment. The Church's dignity of Archdeacon went with the CG appointment and the Archbishop greeted me with 'Are you now an Archdeacon?' I replied 'Sir, I am bogus without your approval!' Pat and I were invited to lunch with him and Mrs Fisher at Lambeth Palace a week or two later. They both were charmingly informal and kind and the Archbishop took me down to his chapel after lunch to commission me in prayer. He then took me to his study where I had advice and counsel, in which he raised the subject of churchmanship. The Department had firm regulations regarding the wearing of robes and the conduct of services so that, ministering to large number of soldiers with little church background, we would not confuse our congregations and would not be distressful to those whose Christian practice of worship leant to either High or Low traditions. Chaplains, however, were totally free in preaching and teaching.

'I know' the Archbishop said, 'that some of your chaplains are very keen to be allowed to wear Mass vestments. Are you going to allow this?' I said no because I was not willing to abandon our policy of *Via Media* which had heretofore held us together. Fragmentation would be the outcome of our allowing different forms of worship from church to church. In service life – unlike civilian life – there were very many places where our garrison churches were the only possible place of worship available. The Archbishop asked if I would agree to nominate certain churches as 'vestment churches'. I pointed out how this would add impossible difficulties to a fair posting of chaplains and that I would never want a chaplain to be compelled to take what would be to him a false stance. Finally, he said 'If I, as your Archbishop, were to ask you to nominate certain churches as vestment churches, what would you say?' I replied that knowing his reputation for total fairness I would ask him which churches should be nominated as 'North end. Scarf and hood' (the opposite end of the spectrum). He threw his arms up and said 'All right, you win'. I loved that man and thanked God for his leadership.

Wherever I went on official visits to commands and Districts I met with generous concern for and appreciation of the chaplain's work. The Christian voice was being heard and heeded and very, very seldom was there criticism. Annual confidential reports with final comment from Commanding

Officers and General Commanders in Chief included such remarks as 'I would feel it more fitting if this Godly man were to report on me rather than that I on him' and, by way of contrast, 'if this chaplain were to emphasise the joy of Christian living rather than the perils of sin he would find a greater response in his ministry'.

I felt almost guilty on my first visit to Germany when I found large congregations awaiting my arrival for special services as I arrived in the comfort of a large staff car, and when I contrasted this with what I had known as a less senior chaplain as a rush hither and thither in bumpy discomfort to reach small units with uncertain numbers of worshippers to whom to minister. I felt I wanted to identify again with the uphill slog which so many postings offered their chaplains.

Sometimes unusual situations would present themselves. One was a visit to the Far East which was to include the dedication of a new church in Terendah, Malaya, the building of which had not been completed. I had not been able to re-schedule my visit but we adapted the situation to the truth that since we offered ourselves rough-hewn to our God that we might grow as Christians so we could offer our church likewise, a place for God's blessing.

Another and unhappy problem arose at home in England. A Cavalry CO went so far as to require his chaplain to re-write the prayer book to make it more understandable. This brought into conflict the sincerity of care on the part of the CO, even if he had overlooked the normal usage of the churches' liturgy at home and abroad, and the firm loyalty of his chaplain to it. Between them the situation, not being well managed, grew into a clash of personalities and finally to a hostility which was harmful to the regiment. I was asked by the Army Commander to remove the chaplain who – perhaps in an unwise manner – had 'stood up' to his CO. Finally we agreed that both CO and chaplain had to be posted but without disgrace to either. I sincerely hope this did not harm the officer's career, for he was undoubtedly a good man.

It was a wonderful experience as well as a humbling one to meet and to get to know so many of our finest officers, both in retirement after the war and currently still serving. So many were of rare and wonderful character. I asked one in high command after he had disclosed his faith openly and whom I had known in phoney-war days as a subaltern 'When did your faith become so real?' He said it had come with the 'responsibility of command'.

I had an amusing incident with Monty. I was on the railway platform at Waterloo when I heard the familiar voice 'Padre' from some yards away. He and I were travelling on the same train. We chatted and I saw him into his carriage taking my departure just before the train moved off. He looked surprised. Some six months later I was consecrating and he was presenting new 'Colours' to the Warwickshire Regiment at Coventry. When we talked I said that the last time we had met I had but seen him into his carriage while I went into another. He said 'Yes, but why?' and I had to admit I was travelling second class because I was travelling at my own expense.

At services of Consecration of Colours we always prayed for our Queen. Frequently she herself presented the Colours and I found it very moving to pray for her in public and in her presence. She always had all the chaplains on parade presented to her, which they greatly appreciated, and on an early occasion I quite forgot the Duke of Edinburgh was accompanying her. 'Good morning' said a quiet voice very close to my ear – I think the Duke enjoyed my embarrassment.

When occasion demanded the Duke could be distant and stern but he could also be totally relaxed. As the Queen and he left a small gathering on Smiths Lawn Windsor when we all had been on our 'best behaviour' he stepped back from the royal car and said 'You can enjoy yourselves now'! I feel sure the Queen was able to appreciate the humour.

Pat and I were at a cocktail party of the ACG Eastern Command in his house near Hampton Court. Somebody came to me with a special delivery letter bearing the royal cipher. I was slipping it into my pocket, trying to hide my surprise and curiosity, when my hostess said 'Do open it; you must open it.' I was breath-taken, it was a Royal Command to Pat and me to dinner at Buckingham Palace – an informal dinner party, it was called.

We met up with 'Chips' (Sir Charles) Maclean and his wife on arrival. 'Chips' was later to become Comptroller of Buckingham Palace and still later to succeed to a peerage. His wife greeted Pat with 'snap' for both were wearing, with only small amendments, the dresses that they had each worn (different, of course, from one another) a few weeks previously at a banquet at Holyrood House in Edinburgh. As we mounted the staircase I said to Chips 'I'm out of my depth, you probably know your way round here better'. 'No,' he said 'no more than you . . . investitures only.' The ante-room into which we were shown (Pat and I were two of sixteen guests) was being furnished with guests when General Ted

Colquhoun came in, looked round, and said 'Ivan, I've never been so glad to see you in my life . . . I'm scared stiff'. He had been my GOC when we were at Catterick and it was indeed good to see him. The guests of honour, Abdul Tutu Abda Karma of Malaya and the Begum of Pakistan, were charming. Soon we were asked to form an informal semi-circle so that we might be presented one by one to the Queen and Prince Philip. I think we all felt very relaxed, but very privileged too. Those in livery who served us at table were in the shadows for the room was lit only by the candles on the exquisitely polished table. A week or two before I had been preaching to the Welsh Guards and Prince Philip was there. To lighten what I feared was becoming a somewhat stodgy sermon I mentioned a recent incident high-lighted in the evening papers when a Club porter was bitten by a monkey in the zoo. I was a member of that Club and had asked the Hall Porter how the man was 'Why, do you know him?' 'No,' I said, 'why?' – 'If you knew that porter you'd be asking how the monkey was!'

I was talking after dinner to the Queen when Prince Philip came up and said to her 'The CG told a splendid story in his sermon a fortnight ago about a monkey!' 'I know,' she said 'you told me.' 'Yes,' he replied 'but I was at the zoo this morning and I worked it off.' 'Oh, and how did that go down?' she asked.

Both my OBE and later CB were awarded me at Buckingham Palace and at the latter, when not in queue for decoration, we were seated immediately behind and next in sequence to those to be dubbed Knights Bachelor. Pat, 'Tricia and Robert were with me and immediately in front was Gerald Nabarro. 'Robert,' he said 'are you going to go into the army?' 'Yes, sir.' 'What regiment?' 'The Chaplains' Department' – Nabarro's face was a picture.

Robert, who had been head-boy at his prep school, was now at Wellington and soon to be head of college. We had never suggested ordination to him in case he felt pressurised, but Ted Aldrich-Blake, his prep school Headmaster, had told me in front of him that this was his intention. This, however, was not to be. He had and has a lovely and understanding faith but when at Wellington he went with two friends on a schoolboys' ordination 'course' at Christ's College, Cambridge he was deeply disturbed. 'Daddy,' he asked on return 'don't they want us to be ordained?' They had had portrayed to them a dying job and they had been told that public schoolboys were not wanted. Both he and his friends have been highly successful in other professions (one commanded the Life Guards). I believe that some valuable service was lost to the ordained ministry.

I had been preaching a worldwide Remembrance Day Sermon at the Guards Chapel and was surrounded by, I think, sixteen microphones between which I had to take a central position. I was given a voice level test. Leaving the chapel an Australian visitor told me that 'that was no sermon' for I should have been ready to shout and to throw my arms about! What a mess if I had done so but, please God, the sermon was what had been given me in prayer and thought. An Old Testament text has always been very meaningful to me 'Must I not take heed to speak that which the Lord has put in my mouth'.

The re-dedication of the Guards' Chapel posed its joys and its problems. Army churches are not normally consecrated because to consecrate is to give land and building for ever to God. In the army we dedicate. Again, to consecrate a church is an episcopal privilege and it designates that church as Church of England. The Guards' Chapel is the chapel of the whole Brigade of Guards (now the Household Division). It has always included the Church of Scotland and I was having it made available to the Roman Catholics for special services such as weddings and funerals. General John Nelson was commanding the Household troops at this time and he told me he had been talking to the Archbishop (Michael Ramsay was then at Canterbury) and had asked if he would grace the occasion. 'Aren't you pleased?' he said, for I must have appeared unenthusiastic. 'You've put me on the spot' I said. I cannot ask the Archbishop to consecrate, I explained, and as CG, I or some very senior chaplain, must dedicate because a serving chaplain represents all denominations. 'I shall feel like a bicycle at a motor show' I said!

The Archbishop was fully understanding and was intrigued to see how I would handle the situation. I invited his chaplain – now Bishop Kennedy.to lunch and we planned proper honours for the Archbishop and that I should conduct the dedicatory prayers and then I would address the Archbishop – 'Most Reverend Father in God, will you pray God's blessing upon what we how have dedicated' He got the trumpets and everybody was happy. It was a wonderful service.

My appointment was of four years' duration and I was asked to extend, but I explained that if I were to stay too long I would upset the pyramid of chaplains' promotions right down the line. I said one year would be happy and probably best, but two years would not be impossible. I was given a two year extension.

Six years as Chaplain General were packed full of challenge and activity. Victor Pike had had a corner enclosed in the Chaplain General's fairly large office in Lansdown House to provide a space for prayer. Most days my Deputy and I would use this together as we knew our dependence on our Lord for wisdom and understanding and sought to pray for chaplains on the ground. It was a place also, in which I could pray with chaplains who came to see me in difficult circumstances and I often thanked God for what Victor had provided.

Some interviews were happy, some obviously more diffi-cult. On one occasion I had to summon a chaplain who had a really shocking annual personal report. He came into the office expecting the worst, but this report of his was not in character with reports which had come in during previous years. When I said to him 'Sit down and tell me all about it' the relief on his face was dramatic. His Commanding Officer was very much at fault and I don't want to say any more. On another occasion a belligerent chaplain came to interview me. I had posted him to Aden and he thought himself worthy of Sandhurst. He thought he would be wasted in Aden. After he had run short of breath I showed him a letter I had received from the General Officer Commanding in Aden disclosing the quality of chaplain he hoped I might send him. He was speechless (and almost repentant). He did not want to go abroad for he and his wife had a nice house in Kensington and she, he said, was far from well. Sadly, she was far from well with cancer, but this he did not know until I had called for a medical report. Only once did I have an unworthy chaplain

who was of interest to the police and whose devious character had just become known in his unit. This was truly
unhappy and was a case of 'Your resignation papers are on the
table, available for your signature or you go forward for Court
Martial and public disgrace'. His home was very close to that
of a dear bishop friend who undertook to minister to him.

It was no joy to have such powers over the lives of others
and it often put a reserve between me and chaplains lest I
should favour, or seem to favour, those who had been close
friends. 'Why hasn't Ivan promoted me? We've been friends
for years' one disappointed chaplain once said. On the other
hand, there were those who once close stood their distance so
as not to appear to abuse friendship. I was blessed by two outstanding Deputy Chaplain Generals in turn. Norman McLean
(Church of Scotland) was the first who, when he retired back
to Scotland, was the occasion of a letter to me from the local
Laird. He wrote that Norman had 'brought sunshine to a
shadowed place' and asked if I had an Anglican who could do
the same for a neighbouring district. It would, he went on to
write, be an added bonus if his name happened to be that of
a local clan! The second was Dr David Henderson, an Irish
Presbyterian, who never gave less than his best. It was a joy
and a privilege to work with them both. We considered
together amongst other things the matters of posting (where
a chaplain should serve), the evaluation of requirements of
army stations where chaplains would serve. Promotions were
the responsibility of a Board consisting of all ACGs under my
chairmanship and with a senior member of the Military
Secretariat present. The most senior promotions to the rank of
ACG was a smaller Board of Chaplain General, Deputy

Chaplain General, Military Secretariat representative and Assistant Under Secretary of State for War.

A huge proportion of my time was spent in visiting chaplains on station world-wide. The first tour I made of Germany I thought to stay with the senior chaplain, ACG of the Command but, happy and worthwhile as it was, I was advised that the Generals would prefer me to stay with them. This was a generosity I enjoyed and gave opportunity for wider views regarding the difficulties facing chaplains and their work.

Before my going to East Africa the GOC signalled me to arrange to stay on after my visit and take the opportunity to see some of the game parks. I signalled back to say time would not allow, and he replied 'postpone your visit for a more convenient time for you'. I did this and Pat was able to 'indulge' there on an RAF flight (the use of an unoccupied place in a duty aircraft at a nominal price). I had to visit Cyprus and Malta en-route and had difficulty in holding onto my passport when changing aircraft at Cairo. Cairo to Nairobi was by Ethiopian Airlines and I was awarded a certificate on the plane as we crossed the Equator entitling me to the ungazetted award of 'Convaricator Shellback Solario Empyrus' dated 13 March 1962.

On a later occasion, the GOC (General Officer Commanding) Far East invited Pat to accompany me to stay with him and Lady Craddock on my official visit to his Command. They felt she would have a worthwhile contribution to make in meeting with army wives. She was again indulged, this time as far as Bahrain which I had been visiting on duty and we paid for her further run to Hong Kong by civilian aircraft.

Six months before my retirement the Church Burgesses of Sheffield approached me to ask if I would consider the appointment of Provost of Sheffield – it was their turn to appoint the Vicar of Sheffield and the Bishop would, at the same time, make him Provost. The older cathedrals were governed by a Dean who was head of the Cathedral Chapter, itself the governing body. Where ancient parish churches were raised to cathedral status the vicar could not be ousted in favour of a dean because church/cathedral properties are vested in the possession of the incumbent (rector or vicar) during his tenure of office. The provost is advised by, rather than governed by, the Chapter.

A previous Chaplain General (Jarvis) had been Provost of Sheffield some years before and I regarded my being approached as a tribute to the excellence of Provost Jarvis. Of course I thanked the Burgesses, but said that I could not consider their offer. They asked if they might write more fully about the work and its remuneration but I wrote back and said the answer had to be no. I had six months still to run and I had not begun to think of what I should do next.

For all my twenty eight years as an army chaplain I had felt it right that I should go where I was sent and go without question, and now I was faced with a choice. This was a very strange experience. However, in six months I was to be 'normal wastage' as far as the army was concerned.

As CG I had been in touch with those who held the patronage of clergy and in the early days following my appointment I was invited to lunch with the Lord Chancellor's Ecclesiastical Secretary (Brigadier Watkins) and later with the Prime Minister's Appointments Secretary; liaison was open between them and the Chaplains' Department. Towards the end of my time these two offices became merged on the retirement of Brigadier Watkins and the Lord Chancellor's Ecclesiastical Secretary worked under the PM's wider Appointments Secretary (Sir John Hewitt). I was asked by John Hewitt what I would like on retirement and I told him I was too busy to think. Would I like a Suffragan Bishopric and I wickedly said I didn't want to be an episcopal curate. (Suffragan bishops are now Area Bishops with their own style and dignity.) 'Would I like to be Dean of Wells?' '*No*' I said again. He was shocked and asked 'Why, it is one of the finest deaneries in the country?' I, of course, agreed, but said (1) I didn't know it was becoming vacant, and (2) I did not want to become bound to a daily repetition of choir 'offices', of which I feared the good Lord might be weary. He asked me what I would really like and I said I would like still to minister to resident peoples with whom I would live and work and worship. I told him of Sheffield's approach and that despite my having stood back twice they had invited Pat and me to lunch. He said 'Why not go?' He thought they had their eyes on somebody else but I should go nevertheless.

Chapter XVI

SHEFFIELD

By this time I was becoming a little anxious about my future for the last thing I wanted was to say, at the age of fifty-four, 'well, that's it. I can relax and do nothing'. I had begun to think that to accept the first thing that came along was healthier than trying to pick and choose.

Outside interests and committee work lay in the Bible Reading Fellowship (in which I became Executive Chairman) the Intercontinental Church Society (both of which were then in London) and I was Chairman of Governors of Monkton Combe School in Bath and of St Mary's College of Education in Cheltenham. Added to this we had a holiday cottage in Co. Wexford on the south coast of Ireland where the Irish Sea and the Atlantic Ocean meet. On our return from Egypt we had bought a tumble-down cottage in a waste area only a few yards from the sandy shore and looking out towards Tuskar lighthouse. The cottage was one-and-a-half up and one-and-a-half down and had no facilities. Seventy-four pounds transferred this and its third acre property to me and on army leave we had the greatest fun in making it habitable. But it was too small and we wanted more room for our young people's friends. Under the advice of my Irish solicitor and friend, Fintan O'Connor, we bought another cottage nearby which had just had water partially laid on and had enough space and outhousing for all our needs. This now belongs to Robert and he has given it a really impressive face-lift.

Irish holidays with the family were of enormous joy, but we felt that these must not influence our next sphere of ministry.

We accepted the invitation to lunch in Sheffield but were prejudiced against going to an industrial city, even if it was in part of Yorkshire. Pat lost her shoe as we climbed down onto the station platform (the only time in her life she had done this) and I hooked it up from the rail track by the handle of her umbrella before we found our way to the Victoria Hotel. We laughingly asked ourselves whether the dropping of her shoe had any significance.

Lunch was a relaxed and most enjoyable occasion and, when coffee came, the Diocesan Registrar came and sat beside me – he was wearing a Household Cavalry tie – and he said 'I must tell you I am against this appointment, but only on the grounds of timing', 'But that makes two of us' I replied. He laughed and asked why did I think they had invited us to lunch. I said that Pat and I had discussed this question and thought that perhaps they wanted a second string to their bow in case there should be any hiatus.

We were taken off to the cathedral where the Church Burgesses had – by long tradition – a small but pleasant vestry of their own and we each, to our surprise, were interviewed. Pat, of course, won their hearts without meaning to, and I asked them questions as well as vice versa. Why did they need the expensive extension to the cathedral which was in process of building, was this for the prestige of Sheffield or for the better service of God? Finally, having impressed on me the importance of the appointment they asked what would I say if I were offered it. Here, I fear, I lacked proper courtesy and said 'Gentlemen, having regard to the urgency of the work and my non-availability for six months I think it would be irresponsible to offer it to me'.

On the journey home we both realised that the occasion had more significance than we had first thought. We did not want to go 'up north' and I said 'Never mind, they will never offer it to us after what I said about responsibility'. Nevertheless we felt our whole attitude had been shallow and that we should now, and should have, previously prayed about it seriously. We felt it was fair to ask the Lord for guidance and we prayed that if this was where He wanted us to be that (1) the offer should be unanimous, (2) that timing would be accepted and (3) that it would be acceptable to Archbishop Michael Ramsay, under whom I served.

It was August and we were in Ireland when I got a letter from the Diocesan Bishop, whom I did not know, Bishop John Taylor, advising me that I should expect an invitation to accept the benefice of Sheffield from the Church Burgesses, and he went on to say timing must not matter 'we are pre-pared to wait as long as is necessary'. The next day I received a telegram from the Capital Burgess 'It is unanimously requested that you accept . . .' The Archbishop – who himself was on holiday – sent me a charming hand-written letter of approval.

Of course we accepted, and with ever-growing shame that I had initially been so cavalier about their trust and generosity and I arranged to cut short some of my remaining months in the army. This was not good from a pension point of view, but that has not mattered.

I was intrigued by Sir Eric Mensforth, the Master Cutler, at a reception they had for me after the Installation Service. He welcomed me to the Cutlers' Hall. 'You have no seat at the High Table, you'll meet all these people frequently and soon. There is no seat for you anywhere, for you will want to move around and meet people.' How right he was.

A day or two later I climbed on to the wrong bus and remained on the conductor's platform in order to get off at the next stop. An elderly and dear man and I exchanged greetings, for I had recognised him from the cathedral. He tugged the sleeve of the conductress and obviously told her who I was. She turned round, looked me up and down as though I were a horse, and said 'Well, he can tell me himself if he likes'. I knew I would love Sheffield.

Very quickly I got absorbed in work of a different variety from anything I had known before. I had never before attended a chapter meeting and now I found myself presiding over one. I must have made many mistakes, but people were kind. The cathedral had been the old parish church and it had been intended to rebuild it as a cathedral before World War I. Foundations for a much larger cathedral had been laid (now under the churchyard stretching out to the main road and facing the Cutlers' Hall) but money had run out. I believe some of it had been diverted into the hands of Bishop Hunter who had thrown his energies into the building of new churches in the Diocese. Perhaps he was right not to give priority to the cathedral, but he stripped it and the provost of monies to which they had been entitled. The Nicholson plans were abandoned and Basil Spence was entrusted to come up with compromise plans between the grandeur of the Nicholson concept and 'modernity'. His plans were not well received. Plans were then submitted by Messrs Anson & Bailey which would extend the cathedral rather than rebuild it, and yet would incorporate the fine Nicholson work which was already in use. The cathedral fund had lost its glamour by now and the outstanding £50,000 estimate for completion of the Anson & Bailey work was hard to find. This was a lot of money in 1966. The Church Burgesses had told me, however, that this money would be raised before my arrival. This was not to be and I went down to London to meet with the Quantity Surveyor who gave me a revised estimate for £85,000. Sir Stuart Goodwin invited me to call on him and he was horrified to hear the extent of the revised estimate. Lady Goodwin and he had planned to present me with £25,000 each for, he said, it was not fair to face a new provost with such a cathedral debt. I was amazed at his generosity, which now seemed to be in jeopardy, and told him I had agreed some modifications which would reduce the bill to £80,000. He said that if I could raise the difference of £30,000 then he and his wife would give the £50,000. How long did I think it would take. I asked if I might go public about his generosity and then said six weeks. He was horrified. I didn't know Sheffield, etc. I replied that all barrels had been scraped and there was a lack of confidence in the air regarding our meeting our target, but I believed the challenge and encouragement of his gift could be used to raise the urgency once again for completion. He told me to tell him as soon as I had the money and he and his wife would make good their promise. I went to individuals as well as more widely to firms and, unknown to me at the time, Sir Stuart used his influence in support of me. Within six weeks we achieved our target.

When I arrived the cathedral was in a truncated state. Two thirds of the nave were partitioned off because of the work of extension and I was very nervous that the congregation might lose heart and feel lost when the whole cathedral was opened up to a sparse congregation, but all was well and the extended building was not to feel 'empty'. Two flower clubs had united to present a really outstanding flower show and this had raised a lot of interest in the city, and an extra joy in this was that the army personnel in Singapore had donated some boxes of orchids and we had them flown back to us through the generosity of the RAF.

One foolish expression of Irish humour might easily have proved seriously mistaken. A dear little lady – the cousin of the famous Albert Schweitzer – took her part in routine flower arranging and I was walking with her when she tripped over the stone step of the lectern. She fell flat on her face on the stone floor. I feared the shock for her and gave her my hand saying 'Fancy meeting a fallen woman here'. She looked shocked and then burst out laughing and accepted a cup of tea.

We had re-sited the Regimental Chapel of the Hallamshire Regiment (a distinguished element of the York and Lancasters) in what Nicholson had designed as the new high sanctuary and I was anxious that what was now a large side-chapel would remain very much part of the whole cathedral for great services. We needed screening on one side, but not a screen that would separate the chapel from the whole cathedral and the architect suggested the officers' Regimental swords would be suitable. This caused quite a lot of complaint by pacifists. An officer salutes by lifting his sword, point upwards, the cross of its hilt to his lips, it is a dedicatory movement of Christian significance. The swords were built into a wrought iron screen pointing downwards – a weapon of war finished with – 'they should beat their swords into ploughshares and their spears into pruning hooks' said the prophet Micah. What would have been much more controversial, if the pacifists thought of it, had to do with the bayonets pointing upwards. These are ugly weapons if used in close fighting and could never been turned into pruning hooks, but they are incredibly useful 'tools' in the hands of men living 'in the field'. The use of swords in the screen would only have represented officers and I was anxious that all ranks would be represented.

As provost I was, of course, quite heavily involved with Diocesan committees and often on matters where I had had no experience, some I attended and some I chaired.

Stories abound about difficult relationships between the Dean or the Provost and the Diocesan Bishop but, although I served under two quite different bishops I never found relationships strained. John Taylor suffered a severe stroke after his Consecration and before his Enthronement at Sheffield. His episcopy was not to last long and was to carry enormous burdens. He was totally self-disciplined, determined that his stroke would not affect his approach to his work and this made him less relaxed in personal relationships than probably he would otherwise have been. He chose Hayman Johnson, a great personal friend of his and mine, to follow Robin Woods as Archdeacon of Sheffield and Hayman was consciously under personal compulsion to 'stand by' his bishop. To quote outsiders they could appear quite a formidable pair! There was almost at once a very sharp conflict with the Sheffield Industrial Mission which – even in Bishop Hunter's words – had lost its way. Bishop Hunter was Bishop John Taylor's predecessor. Political forces were at work in the mission and any attempt to de-politicise it was vigorously and belligerently resisted. Before I had accepted the invitation to go to Sheffield, Archbishop Donald Coggan (then at York) knowing I was a likely candidate for the appointment as Provost said to me 'Do take it. They are fighting like cats and dogs'. A deputation had been to York asking for the removal of Bishop Taylor! There was a deep Christian concern in Bishop John in the first place to see the right thing done and, in the second place, to disregard his own reputation and to protect the good name of his critics. When the official report on the situation came out from Church House, Westminster, I asked him to allow it to be freely available because he had only disclosed extracts in the diocese. He said he could not be responsible for the shame it would cause a brother bishop (Ted Wickham) and others associated with him. He agreed however, that the report should be passed – for historic keeping – to Wycliffe Hall, Oxford, where he had been Principal before his consecration as Bishop. Then came the shock of the tragic death of his son in a motor accident in Kent and this was, I felt, contributory to a second stroke.

Bishop John faced me, on his recovery from his second stroke, with a moving but impossible request. The Assistant Bishop was retiring and John asked me to accept the appointment to be his Suffragan Bishop, taking the title Bishop of Rotherham. I knew that to help to extend his episcopy would only invite a further stroke and, after consultation with Donald Coggan, I wrote saying that I really felt he should contemplate retirement. His stroke had reduced him physically but he had been spared anything which might affect his mind. For the latter to be affected would be tragic for him, his family and Sheffield. I wrote to him saying that I would accept the appointment which was then his to offer me and do all I could to support him if he was determined to go on, but that he really should retire. The Archbishop of Canterbury (Michael Ramsay) and his wife came up to stay with Pat and me while he assessed the situation and both he and Donald Coggan advised him to retire.

I telephoned the Master Cutler and asked if he would allow me the use of the Hughes room in the Cutlers' Hall. This was a select luncheon room with accommodation for thirty to forty people. Tom Burleigh, the Master Cutler, said 'Yes, but what do you want it for?'. I told him that he would be one of my guests for I planned to invite the leading industrialists to con-tribute to the purchase of a house for the retiring bishop and his family. He asked me if I knew what such a lunch would cost and who would pay for it. I said that Pat and I would pay for it. Then he told me that 'I didn't know Sheffield'. Everyone, he said, would accept my invitation but would deem that if such a lunch could be afforded then financial help would not be required for the provision of a retirement house for the Bishop. He would invite any names I gave him to cocktails in the 'Drawing Room' of the Cutlers' Hall and would give me the chance to 'put my case'. This he did, and that night we had the necessary encouragement to go forward. The diocesan honorary treasurer, Graham Murray, undertook financial care of the money and the leading surveyor, Mr Riddle, undertook to advise. A house was bought just outside Salisbury.

Gordon Fallows arrived as our new bishop and was exactly the right appointment. He charmed people out of their fox-holes of critical non-co-operation, identified himself with everybody, never compromised his godly leadership and took his stand on the foundations which his predecessor had bequeathed him. I shall not forget his sympathy and under-standing with me when I had to retire and I loved working with him.

Pat had developed an asthma condition which had become worse and worse in Sheffield. Clean air had removed the carbon from the atmosphere, but the carbon had, in the past, 'contained' the sulphur in the air. I believe it was the sulphur which was poisoning her. We had an excellent doctor who could not have done more for her but she was going down-hill slowly but steadily. She had no sleep night after night and the occasion came when I thought I had lost her. When she was discharged from hospital I took her to see the leading consultant in Harley Street who told me I could either bury her in Sheffield or take her away and give her a chance. She herself was deeply concerned for my ministry and said what would she have done to me if she died anyway. Actually, I must admit that by this time I, too, was exhausted and knew that my work had slowed up.

Despite all the foregoing, we had greatly enjoyed our days in Sheffield and had loved the people who were so generous hearted, sometimes outspoken, but always sincere with us.

Nevertheless, the time had come when I had to face retirement and hoped that such would not be the end of ministry. I rang up the bishop and arranged to see him. He was kindness and compassion. He said he suspected what my visit was about and knew what it meant to me. He asked if I would stay to see the sixtieth anniversary of the Diocese through with its great services in the cathedral and he made everything for me as easy as he could. The City, the Cutlers' Company and the Press all made me feel how privileged I had been to be part of Sheffield, and I was showered with gifts including a beautiful painting of the cathedral given to me by the Chapter.

My last Sunday had come and the bishop told me that he had never given me an order which – in law – he had always been entitled to do. 'Would I accept one now?' he asked. He would be present at all services on my last Sunday, he asked that he might receive his Communion from me and that I would pronounce the blessing (or as I liked to put it 'pray God's blessing') on him and the diocese before I vacated office. This was a total reversal of normal procedure and I was deeply moved by his Christian grace and by the significance involved. The cathedral was filled for Matins and Evensong and it was hard indeed to say good-by with dry eyes.

Chapter XVII
'RETIREMENT'

Pat and I had already bought a house on Rodborough Common, near Stroud in Gloucestershire, because of my links with Monkton Combe School and with the Church of England Colleges of Education in Cheltenham. A further bonus was that we were within easy reach of our Irish cottage. London, too, was near enough to allow my continuing with the Bible Reading Fellowship. Further to this, I served on the Committee of the Intercontinental Church Society and was free to help them during vacancies of their permanent chaplaincy appointments, first in Amsterdam for about six weeks and, later on, in Cannes for three months. The latter was interrupted for two weeks because I had promised to lead the mission in St. Andrew's Church, Oxford – part of a mission within the University.

Pat had been gaining strength and she was able to be part of all this new work in a rich way. Work at Amsterdam and Cannes was greatly enriched by her for she had a lovely way with people, and in her firm and simple faith had really ministered among them.

Gloucester Diocese, too, was kind and welcoming and trusted me with two diocesan reports. One was the study of the needs of a new and larger housing estate which was to become a recognised community in its own right, and the other was in connection with the establishment of a combined ministry between three of the city's central churches.

A Festival of Faith was in planning for Stroud in all its Christian denominations and Bishop Cuthbert Bardsley had agreed to be the Missioner assisted by a splendid Presbyterian assistant. Unhappily the mission committee had somehow fallen apart and Bishop Cuthbert had withdrawn. Being still a new comer in the district I was approached to chair the disintegrating mission committee and Bishop Cuthbert agreed still to be a missioner if I would agree to accept the chair. This was a sad sad situation where really godly people, conscience-stricken about what had happened, were wanting to make a new start. The outgoing chairman handed over to me with real friendliness and Christian grace, and everybody was ready to go on positively in mission preparation. In God's goodness the Festival of Faith meant a great deal to many both within and on the perimeter of faith and discipleship: it drew the denominations closer together in trust and co-operation, and it left behind it a Christian book centre which does a lot more than just make Christian literature attractively available to all who visit the town centre.

It was after the Festival of Faith that Pat's health went into frightening decline quite suddenly. She was in agony from muscles that simply seemed to burn away and which perplexed the medical skill of the county. Her hearing was badly affected, her left arm was useless, her left leg beginning to follow suit and her right arm also badly affected. Of course she was now in hospital – and wonderfully cared for – and wherever I went in Stroud people told me they were praying for her. Clergy of all Denominations were very supportive – including RCs – and some visited and prayed with her. Quite suddenly she turned the corner and her consultant told me it was not because of any treatment he or the hospital had given her. I was enormously grateful to him and the nursing staff and said that God had answered our prayers. He seemed indulgently unbelieving, but some weeks afterwards he told me how he had been down to the Frenchay Hospital to re-examine the photographic records which they held and that now muscles which had undoubtedly died were being replaced. It was a long long haul for her but she faced it with consummate courage – despite pain from further quite extensive biopsies – and she never gave up. Her balance was adrift for some time and once she fell into the garden bonfire which, mercifully, was not much more than smoking. She regarded this as funny, but we both knew that it was time for some form of sheltered accommodation. The diagnosis was 'Carnitene Deficiency Myopathy'. I thought this was a clever way of saying 'we don't really know', but subsequently the diagnosis was confirmed with equally difficult additives. Five other people suffered from the same condition in the country at the same time but their pain came on very slowly, whereas Pat's started overnight. The other sufferers all died.

For some years we had been subscribers to the Country Houses Association and since 'Tricia was now living in Uckfield and Pat's sister Betty, now widowed, was living in Reigate we sought and found delightful accommodation in Greated Manor, Lingfield.

We spent five happy years at Greated Manor in gracious surroundings and Pat, little by little, gained strength. She was, however, very vulnerable to accident. Her skin had become tissue thin and the smallest knock would leave her with fearful gashes and open sores. At Greated Manor she continued to have her ups and downs, but was much loved by everybody as much for her grace as for her courage. Costs, however, were escalating and many felt that instead of the Association serving the elderly the tables had been turned and the elderly were serving the Association. Added to this, although the surroundings were gracious and the administrators of the house of excellent quality they were obviously being frustrated by being required to act on an unreasonably tight budget. Pat was worried that if I pre-deceased her she would be unable to afford the annual increases of charges at the Manor and whether – despite the excellent treatment we received – she would be permitted to remain in occupation in the frailty of age and health. With the help of 'Tricia and her husband, Clifford, we found a charming bungalow home in a choice area of Crowborough and felt we had achieved the smallest house and smallest garden among pleasant surroundings and neighbours. The garden proved not so small, however, and was not on the level!

We were sad in many ways to leave Greated Manor where we had become part of the life of the church there and where I was invited to the pulpits of so many churches round and about. We had formed friendships, some of which survived our move to Crowborough, and we had close links with the College of St. Barnabas (clergy retirement provision) which would remain with us.

Chapter XVIII

EVENTIDE AND MEA CULPA

There comes a time when one is aware that one is in the eventide of life, one's contacts narrow down and travel becomes something of a burden, but all this is less significant than finding that the narrowing down of life's contacts has occurred through the death of friends and colleagues and accepted change, too, in so many of the norms of one's younger days.

When Pat and I moved to Crowborough one reason for doing so was that we did not wish to wither away in a protected environment. For her it was gallant, because she knew she was not as fit and that she was accident prone, but she sought and welcomed the move as a challenge. As events proved it was not easy because she was faced with rapid loss of hearing and diminished accuracy of sight. Two cataract operations had taken their toll, her driving had lost its confidence and, unrecognised fully by her, she needed company and constant care. She herself was always really good company, her sense of humour unabated and her concern about others a lively asset; but her activity exceeded her strength. Sometimes I helped her to bed when she was unconscious of her actions, and there came the time when she ceased to demur when I called in our excellent doctor. She was taken from our local hospital to the Eastbourne General in a dying condition where she was unconscious for days, on another occasion she was taken to Pembury Hospital from home unconscious from septicaemia. Finally the end came one evening while we were at supper. Everything turned upside down for her and her balance had gone. She worried about my getting her to bed and assured the doctor and me that she was not in pain, but it was not long before her struggled breathing was eased in sleep. She was totally unconscious by the time we got her to hospital at Pembury, all reflexes were non-operative, and she passed into the Lord's keeping shortly after midnight.

'Tricia and Robert were with me in double quick time and I shall never be other than deeply moved at the understanding way in which they helped.

I remained at Crowborough for nearly two years despite their loving offer of finding a home with either of them, but the time came when it was sensible to give up living on my own. I aged, of course, but I have been able to continue in pulpit and other ministry and I try not to wobble as I follow the choirs up the aisle! 'Tricia and Clifford have been, and are, wonderful in their loving welcome and in the suite of rooms they have made available to me; Robert and Mary also call their home my home too. I am surrounded by undeserved love.

I have written these memoirs at their request but that word

'undeserved' marks all my memories as I look back over the past. No one likes to record inadequacies, faults and failings, but I certainly recognise mine and hope I have not 'built myself up' or excused myself in these memoirs. The times and experiences I have lived through in – so far eighty-eight years – have been of great change and enormous historical significance and a fascinating period through which to live.